ST. JOSEPH, TENDER FATHER

His Life and His Care for Us Today

Louise Perrotta

Foreword by Fr. Larry Richards

Published by The Word Among Us Press
7115 Guilford Drive, Suite 100
Frederick, Maryland 21704
wau.org

25 24 23 22 21 1 2 3 4 5

ISBN: 978-1-59325-533-6
eISBN: 978-1-59325-531-2

Design by Suzanne Earl

Made and printed in the United States of America

Library of Congress Control Number: 2021905411

For Paul

CONTENTS

Acknowledgments

This book would not have seen the light of day without the help and encouragement of many people. I am especially indebted to Fr. Larry Richards, whose love for St. Joseph led him to write the foreword. My special thanks also to Cynthia Cavnar, who suggested the book and helped me to clarify its focus.

I'm grateful to everyone who offered information and, in some cases, reviewed and commented on portions of an earlier manuscript. Among them: John Boyle, professor in Catholic Studies at the University of St. Thomas, St. Paul, Minnesota; Joseph F. Chorpenning, O.S.F.S., editorial director for St. Joseph's University Press; Fr. John Echert, pastor of Holy Trinity and St. Augustine Churches in South St. Paul, Minnesota; Roland Gauthier, C.S.C., founder of the Center for Research and Documentation at the Oratory of St. Joseph, Montreal, Canada; Fr. Guido Gockel, M.H.M., Procurator General of the Mill Hill Missionaries; Michael C. Griffin, O.C.D., founder and publisher of Teresian Charism Press; author and editor Jeanne Kun; Eugene LaVerdiere, S.S.S.; Scripture commentator George Martin; and Fr. John R.P. Russell, pastor of St. Stephen Byzantine Catholic Church, Allen Park, Michigan.

Thank you to The Word Among Us Press—especially to Beth McNamara and Jessica Montgomery—for providing the encouragement and expertise to get this book smoothly through the editorial, design, and marketing processes. A big thank you to my husband, Kevin, who kept things going on the home front and who endured my late nights and distracted conversation with Josephite patience and love.

St. Joseph came to my assistance often as I worked on this book, as did many friends and family members who supported me in prayer. Neither he nor they nor anyone else should be blamed for its deficiencies. Those are mine alone.

Foreword

"*Ite ad Joseph.*" Go to Joseph! These words have been used for centuries by the Church to encourage people to go to the foster father of Jesus. These words originally referred to Joseph in the Old Testament, in Genesis 41:55, when the Pharaoh told people to go to Joseph for help during the years of famine. During these times of the pandemic, uncertainty, and fear, we too are invited to "Go to Joseph!"

As I write this foreword, we are in the middle of The Year of St. Joseph, as decreed by Pope Francis. During this liturgical year, the Church invites us to go to St. Joseph for our needs and to get to know him and honor him as Jesus did. This book helps us in our endeavor to go to St. Joseph and find out who he is, who he was to Jesus, and who he can be for us!

I have always had a great devotion to St. Joseph. As far back as I can remember, St. Joseph was an important part of my spiritual walk. When I was a kid, I used to have in my room a private prayer altar, with a crucifix and a ten-inch statue of St. Joseph. I am happy to say that I have been the pastor of one of the parishes named in his honor, St. Joseph Church in Erie, Pennsylvania, for over twenty years. On March 19, 2014, we built a very large outdoor grotto to St. Joseph, so that people could come and honor St. Joseph twenty-four hours a day, seven days a week! This was done in order to encourage devotion to our beloved saint.

As St. Teresa of Ávila, who had such great love for St. Joseph, wrote in her autobiography, "I cannot call to mind that I have ever asked him at any time for anything which he has not granted." I can also say, along with her, that he has never failed me, and he will never fail you! He will also adopt you as a son or a daughter and care for, help, and protect you!

I faithfully use blessed oil from St. Joseph Oratory in Montreal, Canada, to anoint people at our weekly Wednesday night novena to St. Joseph, and I use this oil on the last night of my parish missions. I have witnessed many miracles through the intercession of St. Joseph! He is the saint of miracles!

In his humanity, Jesus looked to St. Joseph to learn what it is to be human; we too look to St. Joseph to be our best model of humanity, second only to Mary! This book will show you the person of St. Joseph in many ways. Jesus needed Joseph in his humanity to protect him and to help show him how to be a man. We now can go to Joseph and learn how to love Jesus and Mary, as he did, and take our place in the family of God!

This great book is filled with stories, prayers, devotions, and insights into the life of St. Joseph. St. Joseph is not just a historical figure, but a saint of God who is alive and who can pray for us and help all those who come to him. This book makes St. Joseph so real and so close—and of course, in Jesus he is!

If you do not have a love for and a devotion to St. Joseph already, this book will reveal to you the life and power of St. Joseph through Scripture, dogma, and theology. If you already know and love St. Joseph, this book will help you to grow in your relationship with this glorious saint that Jesus himself looked to for guidance and protection.

As you begin this book, I encourage you to ask Jesus to reveal to you who St. Joseph was and is to him. Remember: since Jesus loved Joseph before we did, he can lead you in your exploration of this great man and saint! May God bless you as you begin this journey!

Fr. Larry Richards, founder of The Reason for Our Hope Foundation

INTRODUCTION

Joseph the Unnoticed

Four friends and I were sitting in our usual restaurant booth, having an early morning breakfast. We hadn't been together for a couple of months, so we were making the most of our time by taking turns to talk about what was happening in our lives.

Dorothy had been seriously looking for a house to buy, but nothing was working out. Now the lease was almost up on the place she was renting, and she was concerned.

"I need to find a house," she said.

Barb looked up from her oatmeal. "I think we should pray a novena to St. Joseph and ask him to find you one."

"I have a prayer to St. Joseph that we can use," Mary volunteered. She dug into her purse and fished it out.

I suddenly remembered an item that I had just put in my knapsack to give someone later that day. "And I have his statue!" I whipped it out and slammed it on the table.

We exchanged stunned looks. It was almost as if Joseph the carpenter had joined us at table and was saying that he'd be working to get the right roof over Dorothy's head. "The whole thing felt staged," Becky said later. Maybe it was.

We prayed. And of course, before long, Dorothy had her house.

Many people can tell similar stories about their own experience of St. Joseph's tender care. Many know him as a faithful spiritual friend—a wise and loving guide who leads them to the Son he received and raised "with a father's heart," as Pope Francis titled his apostolic letter announcing a special Year of St. Joseph. Perhaps you already know St. Joseph this way. For a long time, I did not.

As a lifelong Catholic and daughter of devout parents, I grew up with a basic reverence and appreciation for the earthly father of Jesus. That's about as far as it went. St. Joseph wasn't one of the saints I looked to for help or inspiration. He just didn't strike me as especially exciting or relevant to my life. I saw him as a haloed, ethereal figure smiling kindly from a distance, like an uncle you've heard about but never met.

Then one day my husband, Kevin, unearthed a plastic statue of St. Joseph in the back yard of a house we had just bought.

"Look what I found," he said, handing me the grimy object.

I inspected it with mixed emotions. Obviously, the previous owner had buried Joseph in hopes of a quick property sale, as some realtors were suggesting. Not very respectful, I thought, and probably superstitious. But maybe I could take it as a sign of his protection in our new home. I washed off the statue (yes, the one that reappeared decades later at my breakfast with friends) and set it on the windowsill over the kitchen sink. St. Joseph had finally moved into my field of vision.

What do we really know about Joseph? I began to wonder as I washed the dishes. *Is he someone I can get to know?*

Does anything about his life connect with mine or have special meaning for today? It didn't take long before Kevin and I were pondering these questions together. In fact, much of what appears in this book is the fruit of our conversations about our discoveries in various sources: the Gospels, first and foremost; the writings of the church's earliest teachers, the Church Fathers; commentaries on Scripture by theologians and scholars; teachings and reflections from popes, saints, and authors of spiritual works; and the findings of historians and archaeologists.

There is, I discovered, no lack of words about "silent Joseph"! And no lack of relevance either. His whole life, as described in Scripture, directs us to the heart of the gospel message, to the Incarnation and what it means for us. His special mission, which he received by virtue of his marriage to Mary, is ongoing and benefits us all. "He took care of the Child, he takes care of the Church," as one theologian put it. In 1870, Pope Pius IX affirmed that reality formally by declaring St. Joseph Patron of the Universal Church. And within this overarching role are his many specific "patronages"—areas that Christians over the centuries have connected with Joseph's life and commended to his loving care: marriage, parenting, consecrated religious life, the interior life, work, and death.

In the course of learning about St. Joseph, I have grown to love and admire him. The more I reflect on his life, the more I find to learn from and imitate. And so, I offer this book as an encouragement for your own relationship with St. Joseph, whatever that may be.

Chapters 1 through 4 explore the Scripture passages where Joseph makes an appearance: namely, the first two chapters of Matthew and Luke. The Gospel of John makes only passing mention of Joseph. Mark mentions him not at all. Since Matthew's and Luke's accounts of Jesus' birth and early years are the foundation for a healthy devotion to Joseph, it's helpful to read them carefully, with a view to seeing what they reveal about him. In these and the following chapters, there are a few questions for reflection that suggest ways you might think about and apply what you've read.

Chapter 5 explores questions that arise from Scripture's portrayal of Joseph and his relationship with Mary and Jesus. There are unsolved mysteries here. Chapter 6 draws on the work of archaeologists and historians to present Joseph in the context of his time and give an idea of what his daily life was like.

Chapters 7 through 11 consider St. Joseph, now alive in Christ and at his post of loving and building up the Church in his various patronage roles. Because you will always find Joseph with Jesus and Mary, the final chapter is about the holy family. Sources and notes at the end of the book include additional comments and suggestions for further reading.

In *Patris Corde* ("With a Father's Heart"), Pope Francis calls St. Joseph "the man who goes unnoticed." Because I barely noticed Joseph until I was in my forties, this description hits home and deepens my appreciation for the strong, humble, holy man who was chosen by the Father to be a father for his Son. Whether you know Joseph well or just a bit or not at all, may this book help you to a deeper awareness of who he can be for you. Take hold of the encouragement with which Pope Francis concludes his apostolic letter:

> Each of us can discover in Joseph—the man who goes unnoticed, a daily, discreet and hidden presence—an intercessor, a support and a guide in times of trouble. Saint Joseph reminds us that those who appear hidden or in the shadows can play an incomparable role in the history of salvation.

CHAPTER 1

Joseph the Perplexed

"I see him as a personal model because he was a man so often confused and perplexed."
CARDINAL JOHN O'CONNOR

We meet him in verse 16 of Matthew's Gospel—a discreet presence at the end of the long list of names that comprise "the genealogy of Jesus the Messiah" (1:1). It's not the debut most of us would have chosen for the first-century BC Jew we revere today as St. Joseph.

Roots

It's not that we have no interest in ancestries. Right now, millions of people are tracing their family tree. Yet even the most genealogically minded among us may be daunted by Matthew's opener. We're not like his first readers—first-century Jewish Christians, mostly, who knew at least some of the stories behind the names.

It's worth diving into this sea of names though. They contain fascinating clues about the identity of Jesus and even shed some light on low-profile Joseph. In one Scripture scholar's opinion, Matthew's genealogy contains "the essential theology of the Old and New Testaments" and is so important that homilists should make it a major topic of their Advent preaching!

> An account of the genealogy of Jesus the Messiah, the son of David, the son of Abraham.
>
> Abraham was the father of Isaac, and Isaac the father of Jacob, and Jacob the father of Judah and his brothers, . . . and Jesse the father of King David. (Matthew 1:1-2, 6)

Getting down to business right away in verse one, Matthew highlights the two titles that both situate Jesus within Israel's history and point to his place in God's plans. "Son of David" (1:1) signals that he is the long-awaited Messiah foretold by Israel's prophets; he is the fulfillment of God's promise to establish a descendant of King David as ruler of an everlasting kingdom (see 2 Samuel 7:12-13).

As "son of Abraham" (1:1), Jesus will complete the saving plan that God put in motion when he called Abraham to leave his past and become the father of a great people: "In you all the families of the earth shall be blessed," God promised him (Genesis 12:3). Likewise, what God will accomplish through Jesus will be for the whole human race.

We wouldn't be off the mark if we also called Joseph a son of David and a son of Abraham. Jesus is *the* son of David, the Messiah. Still, "son of David" fits Joseph as well, since it's in his lineage that Jesus' earthly identity is rooted. Joseph is a bona fide descendant of Israel's premier royal family: "son of David," the angel in his dream will call him (Matthew 1:20). Matthew insists on this family tie because it fulfills the ancient prophecies that the Messiah must come from David's line.

Joseph is also a true "son of Abraham." Like the patriarch, who was called to set out in faith for an unknown land (see Genesis 12:1-9), he will exhibit obedient readiness to pick up and go at God's command. He will see the promise to Abraham fulfilled when the Gentile magi travel from abroad to pay homage to the newborn "king of the Jews" (Matthew 2:2).

The rest of Matthew's genealogy is a sort of living extension ladder that leads to Jesus. It's a long ladder—very neatly divided into three fourteen-generation periods, its rungs evenly spaced by the refrain, "the father of." The symmetry suggests that God is in control and has worked things out so that the whole history of Israel leads inevitably to the Savior's appearance.

On closer inspection, though, some rungs on the ladder reveal quite a different set of realities: that human history is *not* tidy, nor are God's interventions predictable. The kings in the ancestry—David to Josiah—are a mix of the holy and the unholy. The nine forefathers who appear between Zerubbabel and Joseph are not illustrious; they're not mentioned anywhere else, which suggests that they led ordinary lives. And then there are the foremothers:

> And Judah the father of Perez and Zerah by Tamar, . . . and Salmon the father of Boaz by Rahab, and Boaz the father of Obed by Ruth. . . .

> And David was the father of Solomon by the wife of Uriah, . . .
>
> and Jacob the father of Joseph the husband of Mary, of whom Jesus was born, who is called the Messiah. (Matthew 1:3, 5, 7, 16)

Biblical genealogies didn't normally include women, much less women like Tamar, Rahab, Ruth, and Uriah's wife, Bathsheba. For one thing, these four Old Testament mothers were seen as foreigners. Not only that: their marital histories carry a whiff of scandal, or at least irregularity.

Tamar, a Canaanite, was left childless by the deaths of her first two husbands, two brothers. In a last-ditch effort to continue the family line, she posed as a prostitute and seduced her father-in-law (see Genesis 38).

Rahab, another Canaanite, actually was a prostitute. Her protection of Israelite spies contributed to the fall of Jericho (see Joshua 2). She went on to become the great-great-great-grandmother of King David.

Ruth, a widow, modeled faithfulness in caring for her family, yet she was a Moabite, a people the Israelites held in particular contempt. Her second marriage came about in an unusual way (see Ruth 3–4).

Bathsheba, an Israelite whose connection with foreigners derived from her marriage to Uriah the Hittite, was either a victim of David's lust or a consenting partner to adultery (see 2 Samuel 11).

Another tip-off that Matthew's genealogy contains something unexpected is the disappearance of the phrase "the father of" as the genealogical ladder reaches Joseph. What Matthew intends by this disruption will become startlingly clear, but already it announces a halt to business as usual. It suggests something peculiar about the marital situation of Joseph and Mary and raises questions about Joseph's position as father.

Jesus' family tree includes some surprises and some skeletons in the closet. What meaning does this have for me as I consider my own ancestry?

What to Do?

> Now the birth of Jesus the Messiah took place in this way. When his mother Mary had been engaged to Joseph, but before they lived together, she was found to be with child from the Holy Spirit. Her husband Joseph, being a righteous man and unwilling to expose her to public disgrace, planned to dismiss her quietly. (Matthew 1:18-19)

The story of the most uncommon birth in history opens with a most common human event: a man has asked a woman to be his wife, and she has said yes. It wouldn't have been a private proposal, with Joseph choosing a secluded, romantic setting in which to get down on one knee and pledge his undying love. Jewish marriage was a family affair that took place in two acts separated by an intermission.

Act 1 was a betrothal arranged by the couple's fathers, when daughters were about twelve and sons somewhat older. Afterwards, the couple were legally considered husband and wife (which is how Matthew refers to Joseph and Mary in verses 19, 20, and 24). Though the bride still lived in her father's house and the couple refrained from sexual relations, their betrothal was a binding pledge to marital fidelity.

Act 2, a year or so later, was when the wife moved into her husband's home. There was no wedding ceremony, but the event called for celebration. A festive torchlight procession, perhaps, as Mary was escorted to her new home? A feast with abundant food and wine, like the one a Cana couple would enjoy? Matthew offers no information here. About this wedding, just one thing is known for sure: the bride came to it pregnant.

Mary conceives during the intermission separating acts 1 and 2 of the marriage process. How it happens and how Joseph learns about it, we aren't told. We learn only that he is unaware of this child's divine origins—"from the Holy Spirit" (1:18) is best read as an aside to the reader—and that because he is "righteous," he has decided to "dismiss" Mary in the least humiliating way possible (1:19).

Matthew doesn't describe Joseph's reaction or explain his response to this shocking news, but Christians over the centuries have reflected on his dilemma and offered various explanations. Most of the Church Fathers, the early teachers of the church, took the most obvious view: that Joseph assumed Mary to have been unfaithful. As they saw it, because he was an upright, or just, man who respected the sanctity of marriage and wanted to do God's will, he wouldn't have been able to overlook Mary's conception of a child he had not fathered. Ending the marriage was the only thing to do. At the same time, he wanted to minimize the public shame that this would bring down on Mary. (The law of Moses called for the stoning of a betrothed woman who had engaged in illicit sex, but it's unlikely that this was enforced in Joseph's day.) A quiet divorce with just two required witnesses was Joseph's just and merciful solution.

Other Church Fathers attributed Joseph's decision to awe. Somehow, they surmised, Joseph knew or at least sensed that there was something miraculous about Mary's pregnancy. Like Moses before the burning bush, he would then have drawn back out of reverence, seeing himself as sinful and miscast in this divine drama. "Joseph feared to be called the husband of such a wife," St. Basil wrote in the fourth century. And an ancient sermon explained why: "He recognized in her the power of a miracle and a vast mystery which he held himself unworthy to approach." In this scenario, Joseph's righteousness demonstrates itself mainly as an awed respect for God's plan of salvation.

Yet other Church Fathers attributed Joseph's decision to bewilderment in the face of two seemingly irreconcilable realities: that pure-hearted, God-loving Mary could have sinned was unimaginable—and yet she was expecting a child that was not his. Unable to make sense of the matter, runs this theory, Joseph suspended judgment and sought to end the relationship quietly. "Knowing Mary's chastity and wondering at what had occurred," wrote St. Jerome, Joseph "concealed in silence the mystery he did not fathom." Here, then, his justice consists in mercy.

Whichever explanation is correct, it's fair to assume that Joseph experienced some sleepless nights.

In what ways could Joseph's example of concern for both obeying God's law and showing mercy help me in my relationships with other people?

The Annunciation to Joseph

Perhaps Joseph slept more peacefully after deciding on a course of action. All unsuspecting, he slumbers as the moment that will change his life draws near.

> But just when he had resolved to do this, an angel of the Lord appeared to him in a dream and said, "Joseph, son of David, do not be afraid to take Mary as your wife, for the child conceived in her is from the Holy Spirit. She will bear a son, and you are to name him Jesus, for he will save his people from their sins." All this took place to fulfill what had been spoken by the Lord through the prophet:

"Look, the virgin shall conceive and bear a son,
and they shall name him Emmanuel,"

which means, "God is with us." (Matthew 1:20-23)

The angel's message centers on the identity and mission of Jesus, but it also reveals the identity Joseph is to have in God's plan. If Joseph has ever wondered "Who am I?" or "Why am I here?," this is God's mind-boggling answer.

Like the three other divine messages that Joseph will receive, this one comes in a dream—but not the sort that leaves a person puzzling over subconscious meanings. It is a clear communication that reverses Joseph's decision to divorce Mary and gives him an active part in Jesus' coming. He is charged with two tasks.

"Take Mary as your wife" (1:20). No need to withdraw banquet invitations or cancel that order to the wine merchant! Act 2 of the marriage can—indeed, must—proceed as scheduled, for Joseph is to take public responsibility for Mary and the child she is carrying. The reason is stunning news that sweeps away all impediments: "The child conceived in her is from the Holy Spirit" (1:20). Far from violating God's law, marriage to Mary comes with a divine seal of approval. God will enter into their relationship in a uniquely marvelous way.

"Name him Jesus" (1:21). In a day when there was no such thing as DNA testing, Jewish law based paternity on a man's willingness to acknowledge a child as his own. By naming this child, Joseph will accept the role of father and give him a family. Through him, Jesus will be rooted in the family tree of the house of David, as the promised Messiah must be.

The name "Jesus," a form of the Hebrew "Joshua," means "Yahweh (the Lord) helps" or, as most people of the time understood it, "Yahweh saves." This child "will save his people from their sins" (1:21). Not only that: he will be "'Emmanuel,' / which means, 'God is with us'" (1:23). Here, Matthew is quoting Isaiah, who delivered this prophecy in 734 BC. It assured a frightened king that if he relied on God, his dynasty would survive an impending enemy invasion. He was given a sign: a young woman—perhaps his wife—would become pregnant and give birth to a son; and before the child reached the age of reason, the king's dreaded enemies would be powerless (see Isaiah 7:14, 16).

Isaiah's prophecy didn't indicate that the child would be conceived in a miraculous way. The Hebrew text, which is what Joseph would have heard, told of a "young woman" conceiving. (When the Book of Isaiah was translated into Greek, the language through which Matthew's Gospel has come to us, the Hebrew word for "young woman" was translated as "virgin.")

Who could have imagined that a virgin could bear a son? Who could have imagined that a child born of a virgin would save God's people by coming to live among them?

And so begins Joseph's initiation into the secret of Jesus' life and mission.

How has God guided me or redirected me when I was uncertain about what to do?

Man with a Mission

> When Joseph awoke from sleep, he did as the angel of the Lord commanded him; he took her as his wife, but had no marital relations with her until she had borne a son; and he named him Jesus. (Matthew 1:24-25)

Joseph awakens to a new life. Having set out for one destination, he promptly changes course, surrendering his own plans to accept a role for which there is no precedent. He shows his "readiness of will" toward God and takes Mary "in all the mystery of her motherhood," said John Paul II. It is "the clearest 'obedience of faith.'"

Matthew underlines the energy of Joseph's response with a quick succession of verbs: he awoke, he did, he took, and he named. One thing this man of action did *not* do, however: he had no relations with Mary "until she had borne a son" (1:25). Matthew is making it perfectly clear that Jesus was not conceived by a human father.

About that little word, "until": doesn't it indicate that Joseph and Mary had sexual relations after Jesus was born? Not necessarily, linguists say. In Greek and Hebrew, an "until" clause is not a sure signal that a change will occur after the event it mentions. It might: "Flee to Egypt, and remain there until I tell you" [to do otherwise] (Matthew 2:13). Or it might not: "He will not break a bruised reed . . . / until he brings justice to victory" (Matthew 12:20, quoting Isaiah 42:3). Commenting on this statement about Jesus, John Meier says: "Matthew certainly does not think that Jesus the gentle servant will turn harsh and cruel toward the weak and crushed after he makes God's saving justice victorious."

In short, "until" says nothing one way or the other about the nature of Joseph and Mary's relationship following Jesus' birth. Matthew is not addressing the issue of Mary's perpetual virginity; he is affirming once again that Jesus was conceived supernaturally and was born of a virgin.

Prayer for the Solemnity of St. Joseph, Spouse of the Virgin Mary

Lord our God,
you visited Joseph in the night of his uncertainty,
and called him to be protector of Mary's child.

Give to all Christians
an understanding of their special vocation,
and a recognition of the gift
which unites them with Jesus, your Son, our Lord.
Amen.

—Cistercian prayer for March 19

CHAPTER 2

Joseph the Hero

"Joseph conquered the devil; he conquered a tyrannical king; he conquered himself."

JERÓNIMO GRACIÁN

If chapter 1 of Matthew's Gospel reads a bit like a *Who's Who*, chapter 2 is something of a travelogue. Jesus' birth, which is mentioned almost in passing, sets things in motion and invites a response. The first one comes from foreigners seeking the truth.

Surprise Visit

In the time of King Herod, after Jesus was born in Bethlehem of Judea, wise men from the East came to Jerusalem, asking, "Where is the child who has been born king of the Jews? For we observed his star at its rising, and have come to pay him homage." When King Herod heard this, he was frightened, and all Jerusalem with him; and calling together all the chief priests and scribes of the people, he inquired of them where the Messiah was to be born. They told him, "In Bethlehem of Judea; for so it has been written by the prophet:

> 'And you, Bethlehem, in the land of Judah,
> are by no means least among the rulers of Judah;
> for from you shall come a ruler
> who is to shepherd my people Israel.'"

Then Herod secretly called for the wise men and learned from them the exact time when the star had appeared. Then he sent them to Bethlehem, saying, "Go and search diligently for the child; and when you have found him, bring me word so that I may also go and pay him homage." When they had heard the king, they set out; and there, ahead of them, went the star that they had seen at its rising, until it stopped over the place where the child was. When they saw that the star had stopped, they were overwhelmed with joy. On entering the house, they saw the child with Mary his mother; and they knelt down and paid him homage. Then, opening their treasure chests, they offered him gifts of gold, frankincense, and myrrh. And having been warned in a dream not to return to Herod, they left for their own country by another road. (Matthew 2:1-12)

Matthew might be surprised at our picturing the truth-seeking foreigners as a royal procession crossing hill and dale to hearty rounds of "We Three Kings of Orient Are." He doesn't specify how many travelers there were (Christians considered two, four, and twelve before finally settling on three, based on the number of gifts they presented), or say they are kings. They are magi—wise men whose study of the stars is drawing them closer to God.

The second response to Jesus comes from a Jewish king who has a natural advantage over the magi: Herod the Great, as history calls him. He has access to the Scriptures, which reveal what the wise men can perceive only dimly about the Messiah. But Herod, whose title is "King of the Jews," is obsessed with retaining his power and focuses exclusively on the perceived threat to his own position. With great guile he summons the magi to his Jerusalem palace, feigns innocent interest, and seeks to recruit them as scouts.

Bethlehem, where the magi now head, is five miles south of Jerusalem. It was David's ancestral town, the place where he was born and was anointed king. Based on Micah's prophecy, many people expected that the Messiah would be born there too (see Micah 5:2).

Not only does Matthew confirm that Jesus is born in Bethlehem; he seems to view the town as Joseph and Mary's place of residence. Bethlehem is his first mention of a geographical location, which gives the impression that they have been living here in "the house"—Joseph's house—all along. (Herod's orders to slaughter boys two and under, based on what the wise men have told him about the age of his potential rival, is a clue that the family has been in Bethlehem for some time.)

Is Joseph present for the magi's visit? There's no mention of him, but it's likely. This wouldn't have been a fifteen-minute stop to drop off gifts! After traveling so far to find this newborn king, the wise men would have wanted to linger in his presence. We can imagine animated conversation, the visitors telling of their quest, the couple marveling. We can also imagine

Joseph pondering these events, like the just man of Psalm 1 who meditates day and night on God's word and deeds.

Do I ever strive to assert my power or position in ways that harm others and lead me away from God? Whose glory am I seeking as I go through the day?

Flight and Murder

> Now after they had left, an angel of the Lord appeared to Joseph in a dream and said, "Get up, take the child and his mother, and flee to Egypt, and remain there until I tell you; for Herod is about to search for the child, to destroy him." Then Joseph got up, took the child and his mother by night, and went to Egypt, and remained there until the death of Herod. This was to fulfill what had been spoken by the Lord through the prophet, "Out of Egypt I have called my son."
>
> When Herod saw that he had been tricked by the wise men, he was infuriated, and he sent and killed all the children in and around Bethlehem who were two years old or under, according to the time that he had learned from the wise men. (Matthew 2:13-16)

Herod's paranoia erupts into a murderous rage, and the "holy innocents"—around twenty of them, by one estimate—pay the price. While there's no historical record of this bloody incident, it's in character with what we know of Herod. According to the Jewish historian Josephus (born about AD 37), his long list of victims included a favorite wife and several sons whom he suspected of plotting against him. This king means business, but thanks to Joseph, his plan is foiled.

Another dream, another divine command: "Get up, take . . . , flee . . . , and remain" (2:13). And "Joseph got up, took, went, remained. . . . Have you ever beheld such obedience?" asked St. John Chrysostom, the fourth-century bishop of Constantinople:

> When Joseph heard this message, he was not offended nor did he say, "Here indeed is something very puzzling! You told me but recently, 'He shall save his people,' and now he is unable to save himself, and we must flee on a long journey and a change of place? This is contrary to your promise." No, he uttered nothing of this sort, nor did he inquire the time of his return, for he was a man of faith.

The journey to Egypt was no Sunday outing. From Bethlehem to the Nile Delta was a two-hundred-mile trek, with no restaurants or motels to sustain the weary. Travelers planned ahead; they gathered supplies, chose beasts of burden, decided whether to go it alone or join up with a caravan for protection. But Joseph is given no time for planning. Warned by night, he acts by night—quietly, promptly, resourcefully.

We'd like to know how he did it. What route did he choose? The Way of the Sea, the major trade thoroughfare that ran along the Mediterranean, was the shortest and most convenient; the alternative desert route was arduous, but perhaps safer for someone who risked being hunted down as a political subversive. Did Joseph consider disguising the family's identity? Did he keeping looking back over his shoulder for signs of pursuit? The angel hadn't told him how Herod would carry out his search-and-destroy mission, and Joseph knew that Herod had a long arm.

Fortunately, that arm didn't reach into Egypt, which was under Roman rule but not within Herod's jurisdiction. It had long been a place of refuge for those fleeing trouble in Palestine, and a number of Jewish colonies had sprung up there. In Alexandria, for example, the refugees from Bethlehem would have found a sizeable Jewish community.

Where the family settled, how long they stayed—Matthew's interest is elsewhere. It's on their departure, which he presents as fulfilling Hosea's prophecy: "Out of Egypt I called my son" (11:1). It refers to the exodus, when Moses led the people of Israel out of slavery in Egypt—"my son," God called them (11:1). Matthew applies these words to Jesus, who actually is the Son of God; he is the Savior who fulfills God's promises by leading his people out of bondage to sin.

God gave Moses a special mission and, along with it, all the help he needed to carry it out. Perhaps Joseph was encouraged by recalling God's faithfulness to Moses during his own family's exodus and exile.

What's my typical response to God when I feel he's asking me to do something I don't understand or would rather not do?

Going Home

> When Herod died, an angel of the Lord suddenly appeared in a dream to Joseph in Egypt and said, "Get up, take the child and his mother, and go to the land of Israel, for those who were seeking the child's life are dead." Then Joseph got up, took the child and his mother, and went to the land of Israel. But when he heard that Archelaus was ruling over Judea in place of his father Herod, he was afraid to go there. And after being warned in a dream, he went away to the district of Galilee. There he made his home in a town called Nazareth, so that what had been spoken through the prophets might be fulfilled, "He will be called a Nazorean." (Matthew 2:19-23)

It takes two dreams to get Joseph and his family back to Israel and settled in Nazareth. The first one follows a familiar pattern: told to "get up, take, . . . and go" (2:20), Joseph promptly "got up, took, . . . and went" (2:21). His first thought is to return to Bethlehem. That hope is dashed because the ruler of Judea, Archelaus, is the least competent and most brutal of the three sons who now govern different parts of the deceased Herod's domain. Redirected through another dream, Joseph heads north to Galilee, where the wily but more tolerant Herod Antipas is in control.

The journey ends in Nazareth, which Matthew introduces in verse 23, as if the family hasn't been there before. An insignificant village not mentioned anywhere in the Old Testament or in historical literature up to this time (and not even in later rabbinic writings), it wasn't the kind of place to attract a ruler's attention. This makes it an ideal home for returning exiles who want to raise their child in peace.

According to Matthew, settling in Nazareth also fulfills the prophets' word that the Messiah "will be called a Nazorean" (2:23). It's not clear which Old Testament text this refers to, but Matthew's use of the prophecy emphasizes that God's plan of salvation is being fulfilled.

It's no accident that Joseph has shepherded Jesus and Mary from Bethlehem to Egypt and finally to the nowheresville of Nazareth. God has orchestrated the whole thing. And just as he prepared the Savior's birth through the saints, sinners, and scandalizers in Jesus' family tree, so he has used human events and agents—some of them unwitting and even wicked—to get Joseph and his family to Nazareth.

"It was not you who sent me here, but God," Joseph could have told the two Herods (Genesis 45:8). He would have been quoting his namesake: Joseph, son of the patriarch Jacob.

The two Josephs have much in common. Both receive revelation in dreams, make an unexpected journey to Egypt, demonstrate sexual restraint, and cooperate in a divine plan to save their people. By doing so, they also become providers of help to people in need. "Go to Joseph" will become a sort of slogan that applies to both (Genesis 41:55).

Can I look back on some event in my life and see more clearly that it was part of God's loving plan for me? Do I believe that God is at work in my life today?

Joseph vanishes after chapter 2. Without a word of explanation, Matthew retires the man he has featured as a hero—the second most important character, after Jesus, in his account of the Savior's birth and childhood. Except for one indirect comment—"Is not this the carpenter's son?" (13:55)—he won't mention Joseph again.

Biographers today would give Joseph's story a different ending, just as they would open it with something other than a genealogy. But Matthew wasn't writing biography as we know it, much less a biography of Joseph. His concern was to present the life of Jesus in a way that inspires faith in him as the risen Savior and the perfect fulfillment of God's plan. Other characters are drawn into this presentation only insofar as they contribute to its focus. Joseph does that in a number of ways. Among them:

- He is a just man who, by his respect and love for the Jewish law, prefigures Jesus' insistence on fulfilling the Law and the Prophets (see 5:17).

- He reveals the understanding of justice that Jesus articulates and exemplifies: a sensitive interpretation of the Law that emphasizes compassion (see 7:12; 9:13; 12:7-8).

- He demonstrates faithful obedience, the virtuous action that Matthew holds up throughout his Gospel as the essential quality of discipleship. Joseph is the type of *doer* commended by Jesus; he hears God's word and acts on it (see 7:21; 21:28-32).

Joseph plays a critical and practical role in salvation history by becoming Mary's husband and Jesus' legal father. But because of his obedience, he also qualifies for membership in the larger family of those who hear God's word and do it. Later, Jesus will stress the priority of this kinship over all other relationships when he tells the crowds, "Whoever does the will of my Father in heaven is my brother and sister and mother" (12:50). And, he might have added, "my father."

Prayer to the Sleeping Joseph

O St. Joseph, you are a man greatly favored by the Most High. The angel of the Lord appeared to you in dreams while you slept to warn you and guide you as you cared for the holy family. You were both silent and strong, a loyal and courageous protector.

Dear St. Joseph, as you rest in the Lord,
confident in his absolute power and goodness,
look upon me.
Please take my needs into your heart, dream of them,
and present them to your Son.

Help me then, good St. Joseph, to hear the voice of God,
to arise and to act with love.
I praise and thank God with joy.
St. Joseph, I love you.
Amen.

CHAPTER 3

Joseph the Silent

"Scripture does not report a single word of his. Silence is the father of the Word."

Paul Claudel

"The greatest things are accomplished in silence," Romano Guardini remarks in his meditative presentation of Christ's life, *The Lord*. "Not in the clamor and display of superficial eventfulness, but in the deep clarity of inner vision; in the almost imperceptible start of decision, in quiet overcoming and hidden sacrifice. . . . The silent forces are the strong forces."

Because Joseph says not a word in this or any Gospel, many people have assumed that he was the strong, silent type. But Scripture nowhere says that Joseph spoke rarely or never. It's the Gospel writers who are silent; their muted treatment of Joseph is most probably explained by their central focus, which is to present Jesus.

We might think of the silent role assigned to Joseph as an indication of his participation in what Fr. Guardini calls "the infinite stillness" that hovered over Christ's birth. When the fullness of time had come, he who is the still, turning point of the universe took flesh in a young woman entrusted to a man cloaked in silence. This young woman, Mary, is the focus of attention in Luke's account of Jesus' birth and early years.

In Luke's Gospel, not only is Joseph not given any lines to speak; he hardly appears at all. Is this the evangelist's way of emphasizing that Jesus didn't have a human father? Did Luke have access to a special tradition—maybe even one handed down through Mary?

Theories abound, but whatever the reason, Luke isn't hinting that the mother of Jesus and her husband were mismatched. In fact, what he tells us about Mary invites us to reflect on Joseph in the spirit of Sor Juana Inés de la Cruz, a seventeenth-century Mexican nun and poet. "What must have been the level of a man who deserved such a woman?" she marveled in a carol to him. If we have Joseph in mind as we read, Luke's presentation will help us come to our own deep appreciation of him.

Great Good News!

Luke opens with two surprise birth announcements: good news followed by astonishingly good news. The first is an answer to the prayer of a childless couple.

> In the days of King Herod of Judea, there was a priest named Zechariah, who belonged to the priestly order of Abijah. His wife was a descendant of Aaron, and her name was Elizabeth. Both of them were righteous before God, living blamelessly

according to all the commandments and regulations of the Lord. But they had no children, because Elizabeth was barren, and both were getting on in years.

Once when he was serving as priest before God and his section was on duty, he was chosen by lot, according to the custom of the priesthood, to enter the sanctuary of the Lord and offer incense. Now at the time of the incense offering, the whole assembly of the people was praying outside. Then there appeared to him an angel of the Lord, standing at the right side of the altar of incense. When Zechariah saw him, he was terrified; and fear overwhelmed him. But the angel said to him, "Do not be afraid, Zechariah, for your prayer has been heard. Your wife Elizabeth will bear you a son, and you will name him John. You will have joy and gladness, and many will rejoice at his birth, for he will be great in the sight of the Lord. He must never drink wine or strong drink; even before his birth he will be filled with the Holy Spirit. He will turn many of the people of Israel to the Lord their God. With the spirit and power of Elijah he will go before him, to turn the hearts of parents to their children, and the disobedient to the wisdom of the righteous, to make ready a people prepared for the Lord." . . .

After those days his wife Elizabeth conceived, and for five months she remained in seclusion. She said, "This is what the Lord has done for me when he looked favorably on me and took away the disgrace I have endured among my people." (Luke 1:5-17, 24-25)

To give an idea of the scale of something huge—Mount Everest, say—photographers often get a human figure into the scene.

Likewise, Luke portrays the magnitude of Jesus by bringing John the Baptist into view right at the beginning.

How great was Jesus? Well, next to him, John is like the little figure in the photo, peering up at towering Mount Everest. John will be "great in the sight of the Lord" (1:15). Jesus, as we will see, will be "great" because he is "the Son of the Most High" (1:32). John will be filled with the Spirit from his mother's womb, but Jesus from conception. "Many" will rejoice over John's birth, but Jesus' coming will be "good news of great joy for all the people" (2:10). John will "make ready a people prepared for the Lord" (1:17); Jesus will rule them as the Son of David whose kingdom will have no end.

People of the time would probably have regarded Zechariah and Elizabeth as the more promising parents for the more important of these sons. Their credentials are stellar indeed. Both are from priestly families; they are "righteous" in God's eyes and "living blamelessly" in following his commands (1:6). The privileged status of Zechariah, in particular, is highlighted by the fact that Gabriel appears to him as he offers the evening incense in the sanctuary of the Jerusalem temple, Israel's holiest setting.

But God has other plans. Some five or six months later, a second birth announcement takes someone else by surprise.

Called and Favored

> In the sixth month the angel Gabriel was sent by God to a town in Galilee called Nazareth, to a virgin engaged to a man

> whose name was Joseph, of the house of David. The virgin's name was Mary. (Luke 1:26-27)

The young woman introduced here has no apparent status or prestige. Luke highlights her low place in society by omitting mention of her family, or even her family name. She is simply "Mary," a humble villager betrothed to another humble villager. If they are within the normal age range for marriage, they are teenagers. Both seem to be living in Nazareth—today a bustling, plain-Jane town of about seventy-five thousand, but then a remote hillside village of perhaps only a few hundred residents. Although legally husband and wife, they are in the first stage of marriage and not yet living together. As if to stress the point, Luke tells us twice in one verse that Mary is a virgin.

Joseph's distinguished family background gets a mention in this introduction, but unlike Zechariah, he holds no honored position. Neither has his descendance from the royal house of David conferred any worldly advantages. Like those European bluebloods who have to convert the family castle into a bed-and-breakfast to make ends meet, Joseph has the lineage without the wealth and glory.

How often have I judged a person by their appearance? Have I ever been surprised to find virtue and spiritual depth in someone I had dismissed?

> And he came to her and said, "Greetings, favored one! The Lord is with you." But she was much perplexed by his words and pondered what sort of greeting this might be. The angel said to her, "Do not be afraid, Mary, for you have found favor with God. (Luke 1:28-30)

With Gabriel's deceptively simple, deeply significant greeting to Mary, the tables are suddenly turned. Mary is "one who has been graced" (the greeting's literal meaning). "She is among the most powerless people in her society," notes Luke Timothy Johnson. "She is young in a world that values age; female in a world ruled by men; poor in a stratified economy. Furthermore, she has neither husband nor child to validate her existence." And yet, of all persons past, present, and future, Mary is *the* most favored.

"The Lord is with you," Gabriel goes on to say (1:28). As Mary would have known, these words had been spoken to people like Abraham and Moses to assure them of divine help for a tough assignment (Genesis 26:24; 28:15; Exodus 3:12). No wonder she is "much perplexed," even "greatly troubled," as some translations render it.

Apparently, George Martin suggests, Mary doesn't think of herself in the way the angel's greeting implies—as the key player in a mission of the utmost importance. "She might have to think of herself differently in light of Gabriel's words." (Joseph too might have to readjust his thinking about both Mary and himself.)

The Greatest Good News!

> And now, you will conceive in your womb and bear a son, and you will name him Jesus. He will be great, and will be called the Son of the Most High, and the Lord God will give to him the throne of his ancestor David. He will reign over the house of Jacob forever, and of his kingdom there will be no end." Mary said to the angel, "How can this be, since I am a virgin?" The angel said to her, "The Holy Spirit will come upon you, and the power of the Most High will overshadow you; therefore the child to be born will be holy; he will be called Son of God. And now, your relative Elizabeth in her old age has also conceived a son; and this is the sixth month for her who was said to be barren. For nothing will be impossible with God." Then Mary said, "Here am I, the servant of the Lord; let it be with me according to your word." Then the angel departed from her. (Luke 1:31-38)

Gabriel's message is a lot for Mary to take in. Her son will not only be the long-awaited Messiah, the heir to David's throne. He will be the Son of the Most High and will rule over God's people forever. Scripture had sometimes referred to kings, devout Israelites, and even the whole people of Israel as sons of God. Applied to Jesus, though, the title has a profound and unique meaning. He will be *the* holy Son of God because he will be begotten by God, conceived through the Holy Spirit.

What does Mary make of all this? Her first words are puzzling. She doesn't ask the questions we might expect: *Really? Me, the mother of the Messiah?* Or, *How can anyone rule forever?* Her "How can this be?" (1:34) doesn't have the ring of Zechariah's skeptical "How will I know that this is so?" (1:18). What Mary wants to know is how she, being a virgin, can bear a son. But why doesn't she assume that this will happen after she and Joseph begin living together?

One explanation is that Mary takes the announcement as a call to immediate action. "She is well aware that God does not issue postdated commands," notes one Scripture commentator. "Did he tell Noah, 'In a year or so I want you to start building an ark'?" Believing what Gabriel has told her, then, Mary wants to comply immediately. But how?

Another possibility—proposed by Saints Gregory of Nyssa, Ambrose, and Augustine—is that Mary has already decided to remain a virgin. In this view, her "I am a virgin" (1:34) is a declaration about a commitment she has made and is bound to keep. (A few medieval theologians suggested that Joseph did the same.)

But a vow of perpetual virginity isn't easily reconciled with the Jewish view of marriage, which stressed obedience to God's command: "Be fruitful and multiply" (Genesis 1:28). The ideal was to have many children—the more the merrier. Infertility was considered a "disgrace," as Elizabeth said (1:25), even God's punishment for wrongdoing.

Given the culture of the time, it seems reasonable to assume that Joseph and Mary shared the common aspiration for a large family. But of course, there's no way to know. While we can't get inside Mary's thoughts on this, both explanations reveal her as a young woman who listens to God, believes his word (without having to ask for a sign), and will follow wholeheartedly wherever he leads.

In Old Testament birth announcements, the angel never hangs around for a response. Now, however, with life-and-death issues at stake, Mary's cooperation is sought and awaited. "On your response depends the salvation of all the children of Adam, of all your race," exclaimed St. Bernard in a sermon that catches the drama of the moment. "Answer quickly, O Virgin! Lady, say the word for which heaven and earth are waiting!"

Mary doesn't delay. She doesn't even wait to be asked. History's pivotal conversation ends with her obedient, eager yes.

What similarities and differences do I see between the annunciation to Mary and the annunciation to Joseph? How does each recipient respond?

Visiting Elizabeth

In those days Mary set out and went with haste to a Judean town in the hill country, where she entered the house of Zechariah and greeted Elizabeth. When Elizabeth heard Mary's greeting, the child leaped in her womb. And Elizabeth was filled with the Holy Spirit and exclaimed with a loud cry, "Blessed are you among women, and blessed is the fruit of your womb. And why has this happened to me, that the mother of my Lord comes to me? For as soon as I heard the sound of your greeting, the child in my womb leaped for joy. And blessed is she who believed that there would be a fulfillment of what was spoken to her by the Lord." (Luke 1:39-45)

Mary embraces God's plan with eager enthusiasm. Luke's next scene pictures her traveling as fast as she can to visit the relative whose surprise pregnancy, still hidden to outsiders, has been revealed to her. Elizabeth lives in the hill country west of Jerusalem, in a town that came to be identified as En Kerem.

The journey would have taken four or five days on foot, and Mary would have needed her family's permission to set out. (Verse 56 tells us that she returned to "*her* home" afterwards, an indication that she wasn't yet living with Joseph.) And since young women of the day would not have made such a journey alone, Mary would also have needed an escort. Was it Joseph perhaps?

No husbands at all are on the scene as Mary and Elizabeth meet and are swept up in a joyful outpouring of the Holy Spirit. Zechariah is mentioned but absent; he has been sidelined for the duration of Elizabeth's pregnancy as a penalty for disbelief. His imposed muteness stands in sharp contrast to the women's delighted greetings and loud cries, Elizabeth's words of blessing, and especially Mary's *Magnificat.*

What good things has God done for me?
Do I ever talk with others about what God is doing in my life and in theirs?

And Mary remained with her about three months and then returned to her home. (Luke 1:56)

Another question: When did Mary tell her family—and, more to the point, Joseph—about her pregnancy? All Luke says is that she stayed three months with Elizabeth. Some commentators speculate that she rushed back to Galilee before John's birth to begin life with Joseph and stave off scandalous rumors about her pregnancy. Others maintain that she stayed to help Elizabeth and paid for her charitable delay by being found obviously—and shockingly—pregnant on returning to Nazareth.

Notice, though, that Luke never raises the issue of scandal. In this Gospel, no one, including Joseph, is portrayed as troubled or perplexed by Mary's pregnancy. This doesn't mean that he and Mary were spared some uncomfortable moments. Everyone in Nazareth would have been able to figure out that this child was conceived before the couple began living together. But Luke doesn't offer any information about that.

Saint Joseph, Come to Help Us

Glorious Saint Joseph,
most chaste spouse of the Virgin Mary,
we beg you through the heart of Jesus,
grant us your personal protection.

Your power extends to every need
and knows how to change the impossible into the possible.

Let your fatherly eyes look upon the needs of your children.

In the difficulties and the sorrows that come our way,
we turn to you in confidence,
placing in your loving care our present cause of concern,
no matter how serious or burdensome.

Let there be a happy outcome
for the glory of God
and for the good of your devoted servants.

So be it.

Amen.

—St. Francis de Sales

CHAPTER 4

Joseph the Faithful

"He is the man on the outskirts, standing in the shadows, silently waiting, there when wanted and always ready to help."

ALFRED DELP

Joseph steps out from the sidelines in the first verses of chapter 2. We see him as a law-abiding citizen who is following a government order, at some inconvenience to himself and Mary. Though Jesus will be sentenced to death on charges of civil disobedience and rabble-rousing, he will not grow up in a household that is a hotbed of political dissent.

A Son Is Born

In those days a decree went out from Emperor Augustus that all the world should be registered. This was the first registration and was taken while Quirinius was governor of Syria. All went to their own towns to be registered. Joseph also went from

> the town of Nazareth in Galilee to Judea, to the city of David called Bethlehem, because he was descended from the house and family of David. He went to be registered with Mary, to whom he was engaged and who was expecting a child. (Luke 2:1-5)

The command that Joseph is obeying requires Caesar's subjects to stand up and be counted in "their own towns" (2:3). Nazareth is Joseph and Mary's "own town" (2:39), but Joseph must register eighty-five miles away in Bethlehem, where his ancestor David lived forty-two generations before him. Perhaps he owns land there and must pay a property tax.

Mary is to be registered with Joseph and not with her father's family—an indication that the two are now living together. Referring to them as "engaged" may be a reminder of Jesus' divine origins, a discreet way of saying that they have not had sexual intercourse (2:5).

Since heads of families could usually register their entire families, it's not clear why Mary makes the trip. Maybe an extended visit with Joseph's Bethlehem relatives? At any rate, the census ensures that Jesus will be born in "the city of David" in fulfillment of prophecy.

> While they were there, the time came for her to deliver her child. And she gave birth to her firstborn son and wrapped him in bands of cloth, and laid him in a manger, because there was no place for them in the inn. (Luke 2:6-7)

"Give me the details," I tell my husband whenever he returns from a solo visit to far-off children and grandchildren. "Give me the details," I'd have liked to tell Luke as he wrote the story of Jesus' birth. Exactly when and how Mary delivered, whether or not she endured labor pains, what role Joseph played and whether he was nervous—none of this was on Luke's agenda. Still, these few verses offer significant information.

"Firstborn son" indicates that Mary had no children before Jesus (2:7). It doesn't imply that Jesus was the first among other children. This is evident from the grave inscription of a Jewish woman who died in Egypt in 5 BC: "In the pangs of giving birth to a firstborn child, fate brought me to the end of my life." Obviously, this woman's firstborn was her lastborn.

"Bands of cloth," or swaddling clothes, were fabric strips that mothers wrapped around their infants to keep them warm, help their limbs grow straight, and prevent them from thrashing about sleeplessly. This detail has often been interpreted as a sign of poverty and hardship. ("All meanly wrapt in the rude manger" is how the poet John Milton described baby Jesus.) Luke had another meaning in mind, for even Solomon, the richest of Israel's kings was "nursed with care in swaddling cloths" (Wisdom 7:4). In this Gospel, Jesus is received like the king he is. He is enfolded by—literally, wrapped up in—the love of the most loving of mothers.

The "manger," however, is a feeding trough for animals—not a top-of-the-line cradle fit for a king (2:7). Jesus, who will announce "good news to the poor" (4:18), arrives as one of them.

I used to think of the "inn" (2:7) as the first-century Palestinian equivalent of a modest motel with a "no vacancy" sign. Not so. The Greek word, as Luke uses it, has a more elastic meaning: a multi-purpose place that someone could use. In

22:11, the same word refers to the venue for the Last Supper. Here, it may be a guest area in the home of one of Joseph's Bethlehem relatives.

Houses in the area were small, though—often little more than a room or two built in front of a cave where the family's sheep and goats were sheltered. As Jesus' birth drew near, Mary and Joseph may well have sought privacy in just such a cave. An ancient tradition does, in fact, indicate that Jesus was born in a cave. The earliest mention of this comes from Justin Martyr, a native of Palestine who wrote around AD 150. To this day, pilgrims pay their homage to the newborn king in a cave beneath Bethlehem's Church of the Nativity.

Which circumstances of Jesus' birth stand out to me? What lessons do they hold for me?

Shepherds Hear and Visit

In that region there were shepherds living in the fields, keeping watch over their flock by night. Then an angel of the Lord stood before them, and the glory of the Lord shone around them, and they were terrified. But the angel said to them, "Do not be afraid; for see—I am bringing you good news of great joy for all the people: to you is born this day in the city of David a Savior, who is the Messiah, the Lord. This will be a sign for you: you will find a child wrapped in bands of cloth and lying in a manger." And suddenly there was with the angel a multitude of the heavenly host, praising God and saying,

> "Glory to God in the highest heaven,
> and on earth peace among those whom he favors!"
> (Luke 2:8-14)

All unsuspecting, a band of simple guys on the job see the sky light up with angels and hear astounding news of a Savior, Messiah, and Lord. Why them?

Well, David too was a Bethlehem shepherd. He was tending his sheep—perhaps in the very fields where angel voices sang—when summoned into town for a kingly anointing and sudden career change (see 1 Samuel 16:1-13). Now, in his city, one of his descendants has become the adoptive father of Jesus, the Good Shepherd and King of kings. How fitting that David's successors in the fields are the first to greet this child to whom Joseph has given his lineage. They rush off to him like Mary to Elizabeth.

> When the angels had left them and gone into heaven, the shepherds said to one another, "Let us go now to Bethlehem and see this thing that has taken place, which the Lord has made known to us." So they went with haste and found Mary and Joseph, and the child lying in the manger. When they saw this, they made known what had been told them about this child; and all who heard it were amazed at what the shepherds told them. But Mary treasured all these words and pondered them in her heart. The shepherds returned, glorifying and praising God for all they had heard and seen, as it had been told them. (Luke 2:15-20)

Great joy, great awe. It's natural for new parents to marvel at the mystery of life and to think their child a wonder. But who can imagine the depths of Joseph and Mary's wonderment at the shepherds' early morning visit and breathless description of what they have seen and heard? These ordinary guys are on fire with the good news. They can't stop talking about it. They leave, praising and glorifying God, apparently ready to witness far and wide. Like everyone else who hears the story, Mary and Joseph are "amazed" (2:18).

It's worth lingering on the fact that Joseph too is caught up in this joyful wonder. After all, considered objectively, his fatherhood is ambiguous; he has played absolutely no part in the physical conception of Jesus. Another man might have drawn back before the mystery—miffed, disappointed, or hurt at not being given a role as weighty as his wife's. Not Joseph. And by embracing God's plan, he opens himself up to joy.

The many practical tasks involved in caring for a newborn make it something other than a contemplative experience. But as the new parents tended to Jesus in the days that followed, they must have felt caught up in heavenly mysteries.

Luke shows Mary treasuring these words and events, taking them to heart and trying to fathom their significance. Doesn't it seem likely that she also discussed them with Joseph? Knowing, as only they could know, that their child had been virginally conceived, both parents must have reflected together about what it all might mean.

What is the role that God has given me? What gifts has he called me to develop? How fully have I embraced his plan?

Fulfilling the Law

> After eight days had passed, it was time to circumcise the child; and he was called Jesus, the name given by the angel before he was conceived in the womb.
>
> When the time came for their purification according to the law of Moses, they brought him up to Jerusalem to present him to the Lord (as it is written in the law of the Lord, "Every firstborn male shall be designated as holy to the Lord"), and they offered a sacrifice according to what is stated in the law of the Lord, "a pair of turtledoves or two young pigeons." (Luke 2:21-24)

Circumcision was the mark of a son's incorporation into the community of Israel, a physical sign of God's covenant with Abraham and his descendants (see Genesis 17:9-14). As devout Jews, Mary and Joseph obey this general law. They also obey God's specific command to them: the child is called Jesus. Perhaps they celebrate the event with family and friends, as Elizabeth and Zechariah have done for John (see Luke 1:58-66). If so, since Mary and Joseph are still in Bethlehem, it's the Joseph side of the family that joins in.

The Mosaic law required a mother to be ritually purified about a month after giving birth. This law didn't apply to her husband, yet Luke speaks of "their purification" and shows both Mary and Joseph at the temple to offer the prescribed sacrifice (2:22). (A lamb was customary, but two birds was perhaps all they could afford.) Whatever Luke's meaning, the scene showcases Joseph and Mary's fidelity to God's law as a couple. It also suggests that Joseph—who accompanies Mary, though under no obligation to do so—will always be at her side as her loving support and partner in mission. He is totally "in."

An Unexpected Encounter

There was no Jewish tradition or prescribed ceremony for presenting a baby in the temple. As it turns out, none is needed. The Holy Spirit orchestrates everything. A holy old man is guided through the enormous temple complex to where Mary and Joseph are standing. Alert to the Spirit's promptings, they present Jesus to God by putting him in Simeon's arms.

> Simeon took him in his arms and praised God, saying,
>
> "Master, now you are dismissing your servant in peace,
> according to your word;
> for my eyes have seen your salvation,
> which you have prepared in the presence of all peoples,
> a light for revelation to the Gentiles
> and for glory to your people Israel."

> And the child's father and mother were amazed at what was being said about him. Then Simeon blessed them and said to his mother Mary, "This child is destined for the falling and the rising of many in Israel, and to be a sign that will be opposed so that the inner thoughts of many will be revealed—and a sword will pierce your own soul too." (Luke 2:28-35)

Again, Jesus' father and mother (as Luke calls them) are taken by surprise. It's not just that an elderly stranger has been awaiting their son and declares himself ready for death now that he has met him. They are most "amazed" by what Simeon prophesies (2:33).

Mary and Joseph have understood that Jesus is the Messiah who has come to save the Jewish people. Now, for the first time, they learn that he will bring salvation to *all* peoples. This idea will take some getting used to. As one commentary explains, "Most Jews expected that the Messiah would conquer Gentiles, not be a light of revelation for them."

Also unexpected is the sober warning that not everyone will welcome Jesus with glad hosannas. Addressing Mary only, Simeon prophesies that her son will be a sign of contradiction, revealing people's motives and loyalties. Some of it won't be pretty. Jesus will be opposed and rejected by many, and Mary will be pierced to the core.

And what about Joseph? Why doesn't Simeon address him too? Because Joseph doesn't appear in the Gospels during the years of Jesus' public ministry, the most likely answer is that he won't live long enough to share this sorrow.

How would I describe my relationship with the Holy Spirit? What can I do to be more alert to his promptings?

Losing and Finding

Their temple duties fulfilled, the little family heads home to "their own town of Nazareth" (2:39). Here begin those tantalizing hidden years whose events Luke compresses into one verse: "The child grew and became strong, filled with wisdom; and the favor of God was upon him" (2:40). Alone among the evangelists, Luke does recount one telling episode from Jesus' boyhood.

> Now every year his parents went to Jerusalem for the festival of the Passover. And when he was twelve years old, they went up as usual for the festival. (Luke 2:41-42)

The springtime feast of Passover, one of the three pilgrimage festivals of the Jewish year, commemorated God's freeing the Israelites from enslavement in Egypt. It was a religious celebration, but also the year's big holiday. Crowds of pilgrims—somewhere between 130,000 and 500,000 people—streamed to Jerusalem. Since the city had perhaps 50,000 residents, this was a major break in business as usual.

Joseph and Mary made the journey with a large traveling party of friends and relatives. It was safer that way. There were robbers on the roads and, in Samaria, hostile territory to pass through. Without a word about the family's time in Jerusalem, Luke skips ahead to the return trip.

> When the festival was ended and they started to return, the boy Jesus stayed behind in Jerusalem, but his parents did not know it. Assuming that he was in the group of travelers, they went a day's journey. Then they started to look for him among their relatives and friends. When they did not find him, they returned to Jerusalem to search for him. After three days they found him in the temple, sitting among the teachers, listening to them and asking them questions. And all who heard him were amazed at his understanding and his answers. When his parents saw him they were astonished. (Luke 2:43-48)

Joseph and Mary are obviously not helicopter parents, hovering anxiously over Jesus' every move. And why should they be? Jesus is trustworthy and level-headed, as we can imagine, and the Nazareth caravan is made up of people who would have looked out for him. When they discover that no one has seen their boy for an entire day, however, they panic. Every parent can imagine what they might have been thinking. Is Jesus sick? Hurt? In some kind of trouble?

The anxious parents are surprised indeed to find Jesus sitting with the learned men—listening, asking probing questions, and revealing an amazing depth of understanding. But perhaps they aren't *too* surprised at how he's handling himself; they must have seen his precocity on display at family dinner-table conversations in Nazareth. What seems to leave Mary and Joseph most "astonished" is that this normally obedient and thoughtful son has behaved so irresponsibly (2:48).

> And his mother said to him, "Child, why have you treated us like this? Look, your father and I have been searching for you in great anxiety." He said to them, "Why were you searching for me? Did you not know that I must be in my Father's house?" But they did not understand what he said to them. Then he went down with them and came to Nazareth, and was obedient to them. His mother treasured all these things in her heart.
>
> And Jesus increased in wisdom and in years, and in divine and human favor. (Luke 2:48-52)

It's Mary who speaks up and asks the reproachful question, but Jesus' answer is addressed to both parents (the "you" is plural). Any way you look at it, it isn't the respectful apology you'd expect from a twelve-year-old who has gone missing for three days—especially not in public. Jesus' explanation—"I must be in my Father's house" (2:49) (or, as the Greek can be translated, "about my Father's business")—may even carry a sting of reproach. *Where else did you expect me to be?*

But Joseph and Mary are baffled. Despite everything they have seen, heard, and pondered, they fail to understand that Jesus is first and foremost the son of his Father in heaven and must act accordingly.

This hardly depreciates their holiness. What human mind can comprehend the mystery of the Incarnation: Jesus, fully divine and fully human? Although their understanding would grow over time, Mary and Joseph had to carry out their mission without receiving infused knowledge of the big picture. We can all relate to that.

When have I been baffled or astonished by Jesus? What helps me to grow in my understanding of him?

Faithful Followers

As the story ends, Joseph is referred to as Jesus' father and parent five times. Jesus will be obedient not only to Mary but also to Joseph—"to them"—for the rest of his growing-up years (2:51). At the same time, Luke insists on Jesus' real roots. His genealogy makes the point. It opens with, "He was the son (as was thought) of Joseph son of Heli" and presses on to its climax: Jesus is "son of Seth, son of Adam, son of God" (3:23, 38).

Luke's list of Jesus' ancestors includes a patriarch named Enoch, who mysteriously disappeared after a virtuous life (see Genesis 5:24). Continuing on in Luke's Gospel, we become aware that, like Enoch, Joseph is no longer here. Steady, silent, somewhat hidden, he has finally vanished altogether.

The reason, it is commonly supposed, is that Joseph died before Jesus began his public ministry. However that may be, in this Gospel, Mary is the parent whose faith stands out. She becomes Jesus' most faithful follower. Like the good soil in his parable of the sower, she receives the seed, holds it fast, and bears much fruit (see 8:15).

Joseph too is "good soil" (8:15). All evidence points to his generous welcome and pondering of God's word along with Mary. His growing season on earth was shorter than hers, but we can justifiably imagine him living on in eternity, yielding a rich harvest in an unseen field.

Prayer in Honor of St. Joseph's Joys and Sorrows

Glorious St. Joseph, the sorrow you felt when you saw Jesus born in poverty was suddenly turned into heavenly joy when you heard the song of the angels and saw the glory of that resplendent night.

By this sorrow and this joy, we ask you to obtain for us that after the course of this life, we may pass on to hear angelic songs of praise and to rejoice in the splendors of heavenly glory.

Glorious St. Joseph, who took part in the mysteries of our redemption, Simeon's prophecy about the future sufferings of Jesus and Mary caused you fear but also brought you joy for the salvation he foresaw.

By this sorrow and this joy, obtain for us that we may be among those who will rise in glory, through the merits of Jesus and the intercession of Mary.

Glorious St. Joseph, with great sorrow you sought the Child for three days and rejoiced when you found him in the temple amid the teachers.

By this sorrow and this joy, we ask you most earnestly to help us never to lose Jesus through grave sin. If this should ever happen, grant that we may seek him until we find him again. May we go on to enjoy his presence in heaven and praise his mercies there with you forever.
Amen.

CHAPTER 5

Joseph, Who Are You?

"I did not understand him well enough,
but that will change."
St. John of the Cross

My sister and I tell different versions of the mousetrap story, based on our memories of a childhood incident. We agree on only a few of the facts: there was a big round mousetrap under an old sofa in the shed, and it snapped shut on my finger. We don't agree at all on the interpretation. (Was there a guilty party? Did Mom punish anyone?)

Our conflicting recollections of an incident I took part in not *that* long ago leaves me impressed by Matthew and Luke's fundamental agreement about the events in which St. Joseph appears. Neither evangelist was present for them, although Luke mentions eyewitnesses (1:2). Both wrote some years after the actual happenings. And yet they are remarkably united on the key elements of Jesus' early life and what they signify.

Specifically, Luke and Matthew agree on the following points that touch on the life of Joseph:

- Jesus is conceived by Mary, a virgin. She is engaged to Joseph, but they are not living together.

- Joseph is not involved in Jesus' conception. It takes place through the Holy Spirit.

- Jesus' birth is announced by an angel—to Mary in Luke, to Joseph in Matthew. The angel identifies Jesus as Savior and specifies what name he is to be given.

- Joseph and Mary are living together by the time Jesus is born in Bethlehem, in the reign of Herod the Great.

- Joseph is of the house of David. Through him, Jesus is recognized as a son of David.

- Joseph and Mary raise Jesus in Nazareth, where Joseph is thought to be the boy's natural father. Joseph disappears from the scene before Jesus begins his public ministry.

The two evangelists agree so cordially on these fundamentals that we scarcely think about how they differ. Only Matthew recounts the annunciation to Joseph, the massacre of the innocents, and the flight to Egypt. Only Luke reports the annunciation to Mary, her visit to Elizabeth, the census, and the presentation and finding of Jesus in the temple. Some of these unique features fit together quite nicely: our Nativity scenes display Matthew's star and magi right along with Luke's manger, angels, and shepherds. But sometimes the differences can't be smoothed over. Here are two discrepancies, as they involve St. Joseph.

Who Was Joseph's Father?

I grew up in a family where discussion of local events often ground to a halt as my father and his sisters and brothers tried to situate the people they were talking about within the larger context of their family relationships. More often than not, Dad and his siblings reached an agreement. Luke and Matthew, whose genealogies of Jesus' family tree reach back to include seventy-seven and forty-one names respectively, did not.

Who *was* Joseph's father? Was it Jacob (Matthew 1:16)? Or was it Heli (Luke 3:23)? Beginning early in the second century, Church writers struggled to penetrate the reasons for the differences between the two ancestral lists. Various explanations have been suggested, but none provide a satisfactory answer. It seems that Joseph's ancestry will remain a mystery. Even so, both genealogies serve the evangelists' intended purpose, which is to shed light on the identity of Jesus.

In their own way, both Luke and Matthew provide what my father and his siblings were trying to get at in their own genealogical debates: "Who *is* this person?" When that person is

Jesus, the truest answer doesn't hang on whether Heli or Jacob was his grandfather. More important is the one that points to his identity in God's plan of salvation. Jesus is "son of David, son of Abraham" (Matthew 1:1) and "son of Adam, son of God" (Luke 3:38). We can read the genealogies with thanksgiving because, as Pope Francis remarked in a homily, they show that "God has put himself in history; he made the journey with us."

Where Does Joseph Live?

Is he living in Nazareth or in Bethlehem just before Jesus' birth? Luke specifies that Nazareth is Joseph and Mary's "own town" (2:39) and presents the census as the reason why Jesus was born in Bethlehem (2:1). In Matthew, there's no hint of a census or a journey to Bethlehem. Joseph and Mary already live there in "the house" where, presumably, Jesus is born (2:11).

Which evangelist has the facts right? Or is one providing details that the other has chosen to omit? This too is a matter of ongoing scholarly discussion. What's important here, however, is not how and when Joseph got his family to Bethlehem: it's that this place—David's ancestral town, from which many expected the Messiah to come—is where Jesus was born. On this point, Luke and Matthew are united.

So why the differences between the two Gospels? One explanation is that their authors had access to different sources: both made use of the earlier Gospel of Mark, but each added material from some source unique to himself. Also, each Gospel was originally aimed at a different audience: Matthew's to Jewish Christians, Luke's to Gentile Christians; each was skillfully constructed to realize differing pastoral goals that we can infer only imperfectly.

Despite the differences, the Church accepts both accounts as inspired Scripture. We shouldn't fixate on the discrepancies as we read them; our primary focus should be on what they proclaim about Jesus. As Scripture commentator George Martin wisely suggests, "We should not try to force Matthew's account into Luke's mold, nor Luke's account into Matthew's mold—much less the two of them into a mold of our own contriving."

Can I see any advantages to having two different but trustworthy reports on the same events?

What about the Sibs?

A thornier question arises from the fact that mysterious relatives appear in all the Gospels once Jesus has begun his public ministry. You might phrase this question as, "How large a family did Joseph preside over in Nazareth?"

> He came to his hometown and began to teach the people in their synagogue, so that they were astounded and said, "Where did this man get this wisdom and these deeds of power? Is not this the carpenter's son? Is not his mother called Mary? And

> are not his brothers James and Joseph and Simon and Judas? And are not all his sisters with us? (Matthew 13:54-56; see also 12:46-50)

These "brothers" and "sisters" are also mentioned in Mark (6:3; 3:31-35), Luke (8:19-21), and John (2:12; 7:3, 5, 10)—sometimes, as it seems, as other children of "the carpenter." The sisters go unnamed, but four brothers are identified as James, Joses (or Joseph), Simon, and Judas (Mark 6:3). We find the "brothers" of Jesus among Mary and the other disciples at Pentecost (Acts 1:14). Paul identifies "James the Lord's brother" as the leader of the Christian community in Jerusalem and names him as one of those to whom Jesus appeared after his resurrection (Galatians 1:19; 1 Corinthians 15:7).

While these references might be interpreted to mean that Mary and Joseph had children after Jesus, the Church has long held a belief in Mary's lifelong virginity. Although this is not explicitly presented in the Gospels, one Scripture commentator explains, it was a hidden stream of tradition in the earliest Christian community—"a stream that flowed beneath the surface for some time and came into the open only after the gospels were written." Belief in Mary's "real and perpetual virginity" developed in the early church as an outcome of deepened faith in Christ's virginal conception (*Catechism*, 499).

In light of this, then, who might the brothers and sisters be? Two theories emerged, both of them with ancient roots. The Greek-speaking Church Fathers Origen and Epiphanius held that Joseph was a widower and that they are his children. This is the prevailing view in the Byzantine and Orthodox tradition.

The other theory, which was proposed by the Latin-speaking Church Father Jerome, views Joseph as never married and the brothers and sisters as Jesus' cousins. His explanation became widely accepted and is the common view in the Western Church.

Jerome made the case for "cousins" on the basis of the fact that the Hebrew and Aramaic words for "brother" are not strictly defined and can also mean cousin. Scholars since then have largely agreed, while expanding on Jerome's point. Behind the Greek text of the Gospels, they explain, is the Aramaic of Jesus' day. And in both Aramaic and Hebrew, the word for brother can refer not only to a cousin but to any other close male relative—a nephew, uncle, or stepbrother. (Likewise with the Aramaic word for sister.)

What it all boils down to is that we can't know for certain exactly how these "brothers and sisters" were connected to Joseph, Mary, and Jesus. Since the *Catechism* states only that they are "close relations," we're free to speculate about the specifics (*Catechism*, 500). Are they children of Mary's sister (as perhaps indicated by Matthew 27:56 and Mark 15:40)? Children of two of Joseph's siblings? Adopted children of deceased relatives? Within the range of doctrinally acceptable possibilities are some that are rather different from our usual picture of just three places at the holy family's dinner table.

Catholics in the Western branch of the Church, who are accustomed to honoring Joseph for his lifelong virginity, may find it jarring to think of him as a widower presiding over a blended family with Mary the stepmother. Joseph's perpetual virginity is not an article of faith, however. In principle, there's no reason why a holy widower who accepted God's invitation to a virginal marriage could not qualify as the Virgin's chaste guardian and spouse.

Which view of Joseph do I find most appealing? Most plausible? Most intriguing?

Sensational Stories

In some early Christian writings, mostly from the second and third centuries, Joseph's widower status is a given. These works, which fall into the category of *apocrypha* (Greek for "secret," or "hidden things"), expand on the Gospel presentation of Jesus and his family and disciples. Written in a lively, sometimes sensational style, they appealed to people's curiosity and contained pious details invented to fill out the picture of Jesus' life.

Curiosity wasn't the only factor driving their production. Defending Christian truths against heretical attacks was another important concern. As Mary's virginity and Jesus' divinity came under fire, apocryphal writers explored Joseph's relation to each in ways that provided ammunition for counterattack. The resulting picture of Joseph wasn't always inspiring.

In general, the apocryphal writings have little historical value and conflict with the Scriptural accounts. Though some call themselves Gospels and claim a link with the apostles, they were eventually excluded from the Church's official list of New Testament books considered inspired Scripture. Still, these writings can't be overlooked by anyone wishing to know St. Joseph, for he figures in a number of them. They were widely circulated, says Italian scholar Fr. Tarcisio Stramare, and had "a profound influence on popular devotion, sacred preaching, the interpretations of the holy Fathers and church writers, works of art, and also the liturgy."

The earliest, best-known, and most valuable of these writings is the short, second-century *Protogospel of James*. Here Joseph figures as an aged widower with sons by a previous marriage (including James, presented as author of the work). Those who view Joseph as a widower "wish to preserve the honor of Mary's [perpetual] virginity," one Church Father acknowledged. Viewing Joseph as an *aged* widower, as this "Gospel" does, is like an extra guarantee of Mary's marital virginity—an easily understood explanation for any heretic who would think it impossible for a young married couple to live together without having sexual intercourse.

The *Protogospel* tells of Mary's parents (who are pious, wealthy, and childless until Mary comes as an answer to prayer in their old age), her life in the Jerusalem temple, and her consecrated virginity. Joseph comes on the scene when the high priest, Zechariah, summons all the local widowers in order to find one who will take Mary into his care. Though miraculously designated when a dove flies out from his staff, he worries about becoming a laughingstock: "I already have sons and am old, but she is a girl." Still, he takes responsibility. In later scenes, we see Joseph agonizing over Mary's mysterious pregnancy, traveling to Bethlehem with her and his two sons, and settling her in a cave while he goes looking for a midwife.

James has obvious deficiencies. At important points, it conflicts with the Gospels. It contains imaginary elements and shows confusion about Jewish customs (for example, girls never lived in the temple). But some of the details it presents—the names Joachim and Anna, the miracle of Joseph's staff, and even Mary at the temple—have been taken up into Christian tradition. Despite its flaws, says Fr. Joseph Fitzmyer, the *Protogospel of James* is unique among writings of its type. It "may contain some genuine historical details," such as Jesus' birth in a cave, and is an important piece of ancient Christian literature.

The theme of "widowed, with children" recurs in other apocryphal writings. *The History of Joseph the Carpenter*, an Egyptian work written around 400 (possibly to serve as a liturgical reading in Coptic monasteries), adds that he was ninety-one and Mary thirteen when they marry; its twenty-one last chapters tell of his death, which takes place when Jesus turns eighteen. In the *Gospel of Pseudo-Matthew* (eighth century), Joseph is ancient—a grandfather with grandchildren older than Mary.

The Arabic Infancy Gospel is probably best known for its fantastic stories about the holy family's stay in Egypt. So is *Pseudo-Matthew*, which tells of dragons, lions, and leopards worshiping baby Jesus as he passes by; of a palm tree bending to offer its fruit; of 365 Egyptian idols falling to the ground and shattering in Jesus' presence.

Especially unflattering to Joseph is the late second-century *Infancy Gospel of Thomas*, which was written to highlight the divinity of Jesus. As a boy, he makes birds out of clay and brings them to life on the Sabbath—an offense for which Joseph rebukes him. He heals other children and raises a boy from the dead. When Joseph botches a bed-making job, Jesus saves the day by stretching a too-short board to the right length. "Happy am I that God has given me this child," exclaims the inept carpenter.

But "gentle and humble in heart" this Jesus is not (Matthew 11:29). In the classroom, he is sassy and arrogant. Teachers want to know when Joseph is going to take steps so that his son "may learn to be fond of children of his years and may honor old age." Outside the classroom, Jesus' behavior is considerably more problematic, causing one playmate to drop dead and another to wither up like the fig tree of the Gospel. "Teach him to bless and not to curse," the villagers plead with Joseph. "For he is slaying our children."

One side effect of this emphasis on Jesus' superpowers is to make Joseph look ridiculous. He cannot control his son; containment is the best he can do. As this story presents him, Joseph is just another Homer Simpson, the ineffectual father of an uncontrollable child.

Wondrous, sometimes extravagant, stories also appear in some lives of the saints. What helps me to understand their purpose and discern how to respond to them?

A Real Marriage?

Two related questions about Joseph pop up as we reflect on the apocrypha, on Matthew and Luke, and on the Church's belief in Jesus' virginal birth and in Mary's perpetual virginity. The first is, did Joseph and Mary have a real marriage?

The short answer is yes. Although Joseph's relationship with Mary didn't include the physical expression of marital love, it was in every other way a marriage. They were truly husband and wife, not an odd guardian-ward duo masquerading as a couple.

The early Fathers of the Church were skittish on the subject, though, and speculated about why God had brought Joseph into the picture. Couldn't Mary have been a holy single mother rather than a *married* virgin?

This tendency to tiptoe around the reality of Mary and Joseph's marriage was definitively reversed in the fourth century, when St. Augustine affirmed it. His explanations were later taken up by St. Thomas Aquinas, who pointed to two things that make a marriage genuine. First is whether it attains a "perfection of form"—the thing that makes something what it is. In the case of marriage, said Thomas, the "form" is the "inseparable union of souls by which husband and wife are pledged to each other with a bond of mutual affection that cannot be broken."

No one questions that Mary and Joseph knew this deep, united love. With Joseph's yes, the Spirit who had overshadowed Mary moved into their relationship as a couple, wrote Pope St. John Paul II. Then too, their common mission drew them into a unique intimacy. By believing what Mary had already accepted about her pregnancy, Joseph was united to her "in an altogether special way." He was "the first to share in the faith of the Mother of God, supporting his spouse in the faith of her annunciation. This made Joseph, along with Mary, "the first guardian of this divine mystery."

In addition to explaining why Joseph and Mary's marriage was real, Thomas gave twelve reasons why it was necessary. The marriage was *for Jesus' sake*: it gave him a home and a legal ancestry; it protected him against charges of illegitimacy and against premature exposure to the devil's evil designs. It was *for Mary's sake*: marriage spared her from being punished as an adulteress, protected her reputation, and gave her a husband's support. It was *for our sakes*: among other things, it made Joseph a witness to Mary's virginal motherhood and ensured that both virginity and marriage would be honored in the Church.

A Real Father?

Yes again. And once again, Thomas Aquinas is helpful here. The second perfection of marriage that he pointed out concerns its "operation"—by which he means: Does it attain the goal of begetting and raising children? Though Mary and Joseph never conceived a child, their marriage "had its second perfection in the upbringing of the Child," he says. In this they are like married couples who are unable to have their own children: their conjugal love finds fruition in other ways of serving Jesus.

Whether Joseph was a real father doesn't seem to have been a question for Jesus or for Mary, who referred to Joseph as "your father" (Luke 2:48) For others, though, how to speak of him in a way that describes his unique role has been something of a challenge. He is "father," but with various adjectival prefixes: so-called, putative, adoptive, foster, matrimonial, vicarious, virginal, legal. Behind the names are varying conceptions of the role.

As with Joseph's marriage to Mary, some early Church Fathers took a minimalist view of his relationship with Jesus. Writing in the third century, with heretical attacks on Jesus' divinity in mind, Origen suggested that perhaps Joseph's role was purely functional, and not fatherhood in a real sense. But starting with St. Ephrem of Syria in the fourth century and continuing on with Saints John Chrysostom, Augustine, Thomas Aquinas, and others, Church writers came to see Joseph's fatherhood as real, though not biological. Among their conclusions:

- Joseph was married to Mary when she conceived: Jesus was thus given to their marriage: to Joseph and Mary both. "On account of this loyal marriage," said St. Augustine, "both merited to be called the parents of Christ, and not only she as mother but he as his father and as her husband."

- Jesus was actually the fruit of Joseph and Mary's marriage. Every newlywed is called to be open to new life. Joseph was no exception. But his marriage to Mary was designed with just one precious life in mind. It was "specially ordained for this purpose," said Thomas Aquinas, "that the Child should be received and brought up within it." By receiving Jesus, therefore, Joseph and Mary's union attained the unique fruitfulness that God had designed it for.

- Joseph was charged with naming Jesus, a father's task at the time.

- Joseph contributed to Jesus' conception—not in the usual way but by supporting Mary's virginity, which was necessary for it.

Over time, these and other arguments added up to a general consensus. Pope John Paul expressed it emphatically. It is

> a true fatherhood. In this family, Joseph is the father: his fatherhood is not one that derives from begetting offspring; but neither is it an "apparent" or merely "substitute" fatherhood. Rather, it is one that fully shares in authentic human fatherhood and the mission of a father in the family.

Joseph's non-biological but profound fatherhood—"a relationship that places him as close as possible to Christ"—is at the heart of his special assignment. He was summoned by God "to serve the person and mission of Jesus directly through the exercise of his fatherhood." In a sense, Joseph's fatherly role complements Mary's motherhood. The two are by no means on the same footing, but their marriage made Joseph and Mary intimate partners in mystery and mission nonetheless.

Joseph's yes to God, like Mary's, was a total gift of self. How is God calling me to make my gift of self?

Byzantine Prayers to Joseph

Catholics in the Greek tradition, along with Orthodox Christians, honor the relatives of the Lord on the Sunday after Christmas: Joseph, the husband of Mary ("Joseph the Betrothed"); King David, the ancestor of Jesus; and James, the "brother" of the Lord, who emerged as leader of the Christian community in Jerusalem.

These short hymns from the liturgy used by Byzantine Catholics cut across timelines and invite us to join with the holy ones who have gone before us in the eternal song of praise for Christ's birth.

O Joseph, proclaim the wonders you have seen to David, the forefather of God. The Virgin has given birth. You have given glory with the shepherds and worshiped with the wise men. You have been instructed by an angel. Ask Christ our God to save our souls!

Today the godly David is filled with joy. Joseph offers hymns of praise with James. Rejoicing, they take up the garland of relationship with Christ. They sing praise to him whose birth on earth defies description, and they cry out: O merciful Lord, save those who honor you!

The choirs of angels stood before Joseph in Bethlehem, saying: "Glory to God in the highest!" With them let us offer hymns of praise to him whose good pleasure it was to become incarnate.

With the magi, let us worship him who has been born. And with the angels and Joseph, let us join the chorus crying aloud in a godly manner: "Glory to Christ God in the highest!"

CHAPTER 6

An Ordinary Nazorean

"What does me a lot of good when I think of the Holy Family is to imagine a life that was very ordinary."

St. Thérèse of Lisieux

No halo marked St. Joseph out from the other household heads of Nazareth. No trail of miracles led to his door. No angels materialized to do his planing and pounding. No ecstasies, no prophetic preaching, no inspired writings, no spiritual fireworks whatever are reported of him.

Certainly, the people of Nazareth were unaware that Joseph was anything special. After hearing Jesus speak in the synagogue, they protested in astonishment: "Where did this man get this wisdom and these deeds of power? Is not this the carpenter's son?" (Matthew 13:54-55). Apparently, nothing about Joseph had prepared them for Jesus' amazing gifts. Joseph's heroic virtue was hidden under the appearances of a very ordinary life.

And what might his life in Nazareth have looked like? Historians, archaeologists, anthropologists, and linguists can help us picture Joseph in context, living an ordinary life "totally like ours," as St. Thérèse liked to imagine. And yet, given the gap between modern America and ancient Palestine, also very different.

The Lay of the Land

Nazareth is located in the lower portion of Galilee, in the northern region of Palestine. In Joseph's day it was a farming village on a rocky hillside. It was small, covering sixty acres maximum and counting maybe four hundred residents. It was also off the beaten track, about fifteen miles from the Sea of Galilee and not on any major road. If you needed to keep your child out of the public eye, which was part of Joseph's mission, Nazareth was a good place to be.

Matthew and Luke tell of Joseph and Mary's travels (within Palestine) to Bethlehem, Jerusalem, and the unnamed village where Elizabeth lived, which was probably just west of Jerusalem. These are eighty- or ninety-mile journeys, one way. In all likelihood, they got to and from these and other places on foot, like most people of the time. This was not a hamlet of couch potatoes.

From their hillside perch, the Nazoreans had a view of the Jezreel Valley and the richest farmland in the country. None of it belonged to them. Wealthy landowners ran large commercial estates there, but everyone in Nazareth was light-years away from that income bracket. They farmed what they had, which was thin soil on rocky slopes. To make the most of it, they built hillside terraces—low stone walls that held layers of gravel and soil carried up from below. In them they planted vines and figs, beans and olive trees, grains and vegetables, all of which needed constant tending and watering. It was labor-intensive work that would have involved everyone in the village, including Joseph, Mary, and Jesus. Everyone needed food, after all.

From Nazareth, the villagers could look northwest to the city of Sepphoris, which Herod Antipas was rebuilding in grand style to serve as his capital. It's not impossible that Joseph sometimes packed a lunch and trekked over there to work on construction projects. Although he was the village carpenter, Nazareth may not have been big enough to provide him with all the business he needed to support his family.

Rich and Poor

Like the whole Mediterranean area, Galilee was being swept by winds of change.

In 63 BC, a generation before Joseph's birth, Roman armies marched into Palestine and occupied it. During his lifetime, the empire controlled the entire Mediterranean area and beyond, ruling from London to Baghdad. There were advantages to Roman rule: new roads and harbors, an end to local wars, increased security on seas and highways. All of this created a vast trade zone that opened up markets for a variety of goods. Pottery was manufactured and shipped out; skilled artisans in large workshops produced fine jewelry and other luxury items; big commercial farms like those in the Jezreel sprang up. For people who had connections and access to funds, there were big opportunities. For the little people—about ninety percent of the population—not so much.

At the pinnacle of the economic ladder was Herod Antipas, who governed on behalf of Rome and lived far more luxuriously than anyone else. The only other movers and shakers were a small group of very wealthy, powerful people—aristocrats, the high priests, and others like the owners of the rich valley farmlands.

Galilean residents of cities like Sepphoris and Tiberias—many of them tax collectors, military officers, or government officials—lived at a higher economic level than people in country villages like Nazareth. Remains of the Nazoreans' houses indicate that although they didn't experience grinding poverty, they lived close to subsistence level. Two dry years in a row could lead to crop failures that might force them into debt or sharecropping. So could taxes.

It was Herod who collected the tributes, taxes, and tolls that the Romans exacted. Some of them he kept for his own use: for building Sepphoris and Tiberias, his capital cities; for maintaining his military garrisons; for paying his officials; and, of course, for supporting his lavish lifestyle.

The system fostered graft and corruption and was oppressive for most of his subjects, who also had to pay tithes and taxes to the temple in Jerusalem. All told, it's estimated that the Nazareth villagers would have had to hand over between a quarter and a third of their agricultural production to the authorities. Given these demands, hardly any of them could manage to keep a surplus as a buffer against hard times.

Hearth and Home

Houses in Nazareth were small, usually consisting of just a few rooms that opened out onto a courtyard. Built directly on the surface of the bedrock, they had walls of stone and flat roofs made by laying slats or poles across wooden beams and then covering the whole thing with clay or plaster. Under the houses were cellars carved out of the rock; this is where grains and beans, wine and oil were stored.

Roofs, reached by outside stairs or an inside ladder, were flat and provided a place for laundry, bathing, hot weather sleep-outs, and drying food, fodder, and fuel. Courtyards were all-purpose areas for household tasks, sheltering animals, and baking the family's daily bread in the outdoor oven.

For those of us who like our homes airy and bright, homes like Joseph's would take some getting used to. Doors and windows were kept to a minimum, so rooms were generally dark and close. Oil lamps provided some light, but nothing like what we're used to. We might not appreciate living so close to the sheep, goats, and donkeys in the courtyard either. Or so close to other people. In this culture, personal privacy as we think of it was nonexistent.

All in the Family

As in other rural villages, the people of Nazareth lived in close quarters—their small, stone homes all crowded together and often sharing a courtyard. Their nearest neighbors were members of their extended family. Married sons lived close to their parents' home with their wives and children, as did other assorted relatives. Married daughters lived with or near their in-laws.

Within the family, as at every level of this patriarchal society, men were seen as the leaders and decision-makers. Except for childless widows, divorced women with no family ties, and prostitutes, every woman lived under male protection. Elderly parents and grandparents were honored. "The older an individual, the higher the status," according to one anthropologist.

Maybe that's partly because fewer people reached old age. Infectious diseases like dysentery, typhus, and especially malaria took a toll. Flies and the challenges of hygiene contributed to health problems like intestinal parasites, skin diseases, and trachoma, which can lead to blindness. The infant mortality rate was high, and less than half of the people who reached the age of fifteen would live to reach fifty. Like Anna and Simeon, however, there were those who survived to a ripe old age.

Joseph, Mary, and Jesus lived surrounded by relatives and other people. Is this how I've thought of them?

The Nazorean Wardrobe and Diet

A few basic articles of clothing served everyone, year in, year out. The tunic was a neck-to-ankle rectangle of linen or wool with head and arm openings. It came in a variety of lengths and colors (often darker and more varied for women), and more than one could be worn for warmth. A mantle, or cloak, was worn over it; this was a short-sleeved or sleeveless coat—loose-fitting, sturdy, and all-purpose. Men's cloaks had bluish-purple tassels at the corners, a visual reminder to obey God's law (see Numbers 15:38-39).

Everyone wore a belt: with it you could turn your cloak into a carry-all pouch, or you could "gird your loins," that is, tuck up your garments for greater freedom of movement. The wardrobe was completed by a pair of simple sandals and a cloth head covering for protection against sun and wind; men secured it with a headband, women draped or wrapped it around the head and sometimes also used a face veil.

As for food, like everywhere else in Palestine, Nazoreans ate bread (preferably made from wheat, but barley was also used), and lots of it. It may have supplied up to half the day's calories. Grains were also eaten parched (roasted on a hot griddle) as porridge. Also common were olive oil, legumes, fruits, and vegetables. There were dairy products too, most of them from goats, which are more resilient than sheep or cows (they can graze on marginal land and go up to two weeks without water). Plentiful and easy to digest, goat's milk was made into buttermilk, yogurt, cheese, and curds, as well as drunk sour out of skins. Meat was rare. And since Nazareth isn't near any body of water, so was fresh fish.

Work in the Village

Descriptions of village life in first-century Galilee abound with phrases like "dominated by work." Most people worked the land—or, in Nazareth, those terraces built on rock. Some may have sold produce and livestock, as well as homemade goods, at city markets.

Some villagers, like Joseph the carpenter, worked at a trade. "Carpenter," as we use the word, is too narrow a description of what he did, however. The precise Aramaic word for it is unknown, but in Greek Joseph was a *tekton*: a craftsman working with any hard material such as wood, stone, or bricks. Bricklaying and stonemasonry would be among the skills listed on his resume.

The women of Nazareth had long to-do lists. Besides doing outdoor work like watering, pasturing goats, and harvesting olives, they swept, cleaned, did laundry, and drew water from the well. Feeding and clothing their families was probably what took up most of their time. Bread-making was an especially lengthy process because it took so long to grind the wheat: an estimated three hours to produce enough flour for making pita-like loaves for a household of six. Less appetizing but vital, since there was very little wood to burn in the oven, was the task of making fuel patties out of donkey dung. Salted and sun-dried, these provided reliable cooking fuel, especially during the rainy season.

Linen clothing made from flax was typical of Galilee, so it's likely that Mary spent many hours processing flax for its fibers. She would then spin the fibers into thread, weave them together to produce the fabric, and then sew the garments. "Maybe we should think of Mary the Worker along with Joseph the Worker," my husband remarked.

Has the busyness of my life made me
inattentive to God's presence?

School and Synagogue

Girls and boys worked too—indoors and outdoors and, if they were sons of craftsmen, at their fathers' side. They didn't go to school; there were none in places like Nazareth. There and elsewhere across the Roman empire, not many people learned to read; literacy rates for adult males were less than ten percent.

The main language of Palestine was Aramaic, which children picked up from hearing it all around them. Some Nazoreans may also have known a bit of Greek, which came to the Near East through the military campaigns of Alexander the Great (336–323 BC) and became the common language throughout the Roman empire. For business purposes, you needed some Greek. As for Hebrew, which was the language of Scripture, few, if any, villagers would have known it. When Scripture was read aloud in the synagogue, people waited for the accompanying

Aramaic translations and homilies to understand what they had heard.

In Luke's Gospel, we see the adult Jesus reading from the prophet Isaiah in the Nazareth synagogue (4:16). How would a Jewish boy from the lower social echelons have gotten this training? This is especially curious since this reading of a scroll demonstrated what one scholar calls a "scribal literacy" that typically came from higher studies at some urban center—"the ability to read sophisticated theological and literary works and comment on them." Giving Jesus a start in life and educating him in the Jewish faith was his parents' responsibility—in this culture, Joseph's especially. How did it happen? Did Joseph himself have the training to instruct his son? Did he hire a teacher? Where would he have gotten the funds? Were learned or wealthy relatives involved—perhaps on Mary's side of the family? Many theories have been proposed, but really, no one knows.

What is certain is that Jesus was given careful at-home religious training by both of his parents. They taught him to pray. They took him with them to Jerusalem for the great feasts. They taught him, "on the human level," Pope Benedict specifies, the "steadfast interiority" by which a person lives in constant awareness of God. He pictures Joseph taking Jesus to the synagogue on the Sabbath, leading prayers at home, showing him how to live: "In the rhythm of the days he spent at Nazareth, in the simple home and in Joseph's workshop, Jesus learned to alternate prayer and work, as well as to offer God his labor in earning the bread the family needed."

What's my reaction to the thought that Jesus received training from Joseph and Mary?

First-century Nazareth—this is where the Word became flesh and came to dwell among us. Not in a monastic enclosure but in a struggling village of narrow streets and crowded houses—a busy, noisy, pungent place. Not to a haloed pair who lived in silence behind drawn blinds, but to a holy couple with a unique but largely hidden relationship with God.

Every day, the holy family interacted with the less holy and the unholy families around them. Jesus worked, played games, and ran about in courtyards with the other boys. Mary joined the groups of women making their daily runs to the well. Joseph had friends and business contacts.

This is where it happened—in a setting that was terribly ordinary. In the family of Joseph the carpenter, who looked and lived like everyone else in the village—like ordinary Nazoreans.

Prayer to St. Joseph, Guardian of Families

Dear St. Joseph, in you we have a model husband.
Your love for Mary, your wife, was a loving bond.
With your concern and affection, you filled her heart.
Your words or thoughtless actions never caused her hurt.

Dear St. Joseph, you were such a loving father to Jesus.

Dear St. Joseph, we choose you as our protector. Protect our families from every disorder. Watch over your children and keep from them the darkness of sin. In moments of temptation, show us the way to victory.

Dear St. Joseph, defender of peace and justice, help us to build our homes on love and sacrifice. Show everyone his or her responsibility to preserve and protect the spirit of unity.

Dear St. Joseph, help us to build true Christian homes, where young and old are accepted and feel at home. Remove from our hearts selfishness and arrogance, and bind us with the unbreakable cord of patience.

Dear St. Joseph, show us the merits of forgiveness. May our hearts never hoard resentments or bitterness. Be by our side, whether we are awake or asleep. And at the hour of our death, help us to sleep in God!

CHAPTER 7

A Friend in High Places

"Joseph lives. He may seem far away from us, but he is not."

KARL RAHNER

When one of Cheryl Scheidel's teenage sons totaled her ten-year-old van, she immediately sought help from a close friend. "St. Joseph, you know I have no way to replace this vehicle. Please provide for us." Three weeks later, a parishioner gave her a Honda Civic with only seventeen thousand miles on it. Cheryl was delighted, but not especially surprised:

"I've been turning to St. Joseph ever since I was widowed at forty-three, with eight of nine children still at home," she explains. Led into deeper prayer though her grief, Cheryl drew closer to Mary, and through her to St. Joseph. "As a single parent of teenage sons who needed to tangle with a dad but didn't have one, I asked St. Joseph to guide and protect my family and to be a father to all the children. He has, and I have come to love him so much. As I have meditated on his life, I have been very moved by his enormous devotion to Our Lady and Jesus. I wish to love them as he does, to the best of my ability."

Life in the Body of Christ

Why would a hard-pressed widow seek a dead man's help for her practical needs? And how can a third-millennium American insist that she has a special friendship with Joseph, a first-century carpenter from Galilee?

There's a simple explanation: it's the vision of the Church as the body of Christ—"a living body in which all the members are in communion with one another," explains theologian Edward O'Connor, "an organic body in which the members collaborate with one another for the good of all."

Some members of this body—those in heaven and those who are experiencing the purification of purgatory—are no longer on earth. Yet through Christ, the head of the body, they remain in living communion with us. Dead to the world, they are alive in Christ and, in the case of the saints, more vibrantly alive than any earthling we will ever encounter this side of eternity.

And so, Joseph lives! In Jesus and through the Holy Spirit, he is no longer limited by the creaturely boundaries of space and time. He reaches out to us over the centuries, over the great divide of physical death. He's not just a historical figure we can know something about, like Cleopatra or Alexander Hamilton. Like Jesus and Mary, Joseph is someone we can get to know and be friends with.

For sure, it can be difficult to make the connection between the simple carpenter of the Gospels and the exalted figure we honor in his glorified state. But as we come to appreciate St. Joseph's role in the body of Christ, we'll find that it flows from what Scripture says of him. The saint we honor as Patron of the Universal Church—to mention only one of his roles—really is the same person we read about in the Gospels. In the following chapters, we'll take a look at some of these roles, or patronages. First, though, let's think about what makes for a healthy relationship with the saints in general, and with St. Joseph in particular. A healthy relationship includes three elements: honor for the life they led; taking them as models, and asking them to intercede with God on our behalf.

Honoring St. Joseph

"Why honor anyone but God?" people sometimes ask. One compelling reason: because God does. "Whoever serves me, the Father will honor," Jesus told the disciples (John 12:26). Following the Father's example indicates that we agree with his priorities for human beings and opens us up to the influence of saints like Joseph.

Of course, God alone is to be worshiped and adored. When we venerate the saints, we're praising *his* work in them; the honor we give them is directed to God. Our devotion goes wrong if it fixates on a saint to the point of diminishing or displacing God.

For instance, some prayers to St. Joseph, Mary, and others give the impression that these saints are more merciful than any Person of the Trinity. Though it's God who is "the Father of mercies" (2 Corinthians 1:3), his servants are presented as laboring day and night to calm his wrath and keep him from raining divine thunderbolts on the earth. Other prayers—like the ones to St. Joseph that are guaranteed to be "foolproof" and "one hundred percent effective"—imply that saints are more powerful than the God they serve. If we really want to honor them, we'll keep in mind that the description "never been known to fail" applies to God alone.

There's a great freedom about devotion to the saints. While the Church has defined dogmas that relate to Mary (among them, the Immaculate Conception and the Assumption), honoring particular saints falls into the category of devotion, not doctrine. It's not part of the bedrock foundation of our faith, like the Creed. Certainly, we believe that people who were faithful to Christ on earth now live in glory with him and are rooting for us as a great "cloud of witnesses" (Hebrews 12:1). But we're under no obligation to cultivate special devotions.

Given the benefits, though, it's worth reflecting on who stands out to you in that varied multitude of saintly men and women. You might think of it as dropping in on a huge party and being drawn to someone you can relate to. Finding a saint friend like that is to step into a heavenly Big Brother or Big Sister program, or even—as many have said about friendship with St. Joseph—to find another father.

Who are the saints I admire and feel drawn to?
Which of them would I like to know better?
How might I go about that?

Asking St. Joseph's Intercession

"Pray for us" (Colossians 4:3; 1 Thessalonians 5:25; 2 Thessalonians 3:1). "Pray for one another" (James 5:16). Pray "for everyone" (1 Timothy 2:1). Verses like these show the body of Christ as a vast prayer chain. Its mightiest intercessors are in heaven, in intimate union with Jesus, our great high priest who "lives to make intercession" for all who approach God through him (Hebrews 7:25).

Among those mighty prayer partners is St. Joseph. When you turn to him as a special intercessor, you're in good company. St. Teresa of Ávila (1515–1582) did the same. As she saw it, Jesus can refuse nothing to "this glorious saint" who exercised authority over him as his earthly father. "I have experience that he helps in all our needs," wrote Teresa, who had many as she labored to reform the Carmelite Order and to found monasteries across Spain. She backed her claim with examples like this one, from a time of distress "when I didn't know what to do or how to pay some workmen."

> St. Joseph appeared to me and revealed to me that I would not be lacking, that I should hire them. And so I did, without so much as a penny. And the Lord provided for me in ways that amazed those who heard about it.

Sometimes, Teresa made her prayer concrete by using religious objects—statues or medals of St. Joseph that she reportedly buried on land she hoped to buy for the monasteries she was building. So did St. André Bessette (1845–1937), a

Holy Cross brother who has been called the twentieth-century apostle of St. Joseph. He buried a medal of the saint on Montreal's high hill because, he told a friend, "St. Joseph needs it." Today, an immense basilica dedicated to St. Joseph stands on the site.

For Brother André, just holding his medal was a prayer—"almost like holding St. Joseph's hand," says one biographer; he advised it to anyone who was dreading a difficult meeting or conversation. "Hold it in your hand while you're talking. St. Joseph will help you." Brother André also liked to pray using oil from a lamp that he kept burning in front of a statue of Joseph. Many of the one hundred and twenty-five physical healings recounted during his beatification process were from people who were anointed with this "St. Joseph's oil."

It's not irreverent to express our petitions by using humble things like oil and medals. After all, Brother André used to say, "we're not walking brains. We need to see, to touch, and to feel." The question, though, is whether we're using these prayer aids to get our own way. Take the popular practice of burying a statue of St. Joseph on the grounds of a property you want to sell. Depending on your interior disposition, Fr. Benedict Groeschel observes, this might be "an informed devotion of piety and faith," or it might be "simply magic."

> When affluent people who never attend church, pray, or question the moral propriety of their behavior bury statues of St. Joseph in the garden of their expensive suburban homes in hope of selling them faster or for a better price, we are dangerously approaching magic. When the Missionaries of Charity

put a medal of St. Joseph near a building they hope to get to care for the poor, and back this act of devotion up with piety and perfect abandonment to God's will, it is not magic but an expression of devotion.

Do I see intercessory prayer to the saints as a way of twisting God's arm? Am I ready to trust God even if I don't see my prayers answered—or answered the way I want?

Taking St. Joseph as a Model

Scripture urges us to imitate those who are strong in faith and love of God. Joseph is a standout exemplar, wrote St. John Chrysostom, for "here, 'just man' means adorned with every virtue." He is the most imitable of saints; his example of loving obedience, courage, and trust speaks to people in a wide variety of situations.

St. Joseph is a model for parents and spouses, and also for single men and women who live celibate lives, whether as laypeople or as consecrated religious. Especially, says one spiritual writer, he is the patron of priests: like Joseph, who was the first man to hold Jesus in his arms, "the priest is privileged to touch and reverently handle him who was born of Mary."

Even more broadly, the Guardian of Virgins is there for anyone who must avoid sexual intercourse, for whatever reason:

young people facing cultural pressures to lose their virginity as fast as possible; dating singles who choose not to live together before marrying; men and women who have never married; and married couples who must abstain from intercourse for health or other reasons.

Joseph is a model for workers and businesspeople but also for contemplatives; for travelers and pilgrims, but also for stay-at-homes. Missionaries and teachers, immigrants and refugees, the poor, the sick, the dying, the persecuted, the perplexed—Joseph's example speaks to all these situations and more.

A custodian I know thinks about Joseph as he vacuums, cleans bathrooms, and takes out the trash; it helps him to focus on doing his work as a service to the Lord. One of my grandsons, a talkative person, reflects on a point that Fr. Larry Richards made in an online conference for men: as the Gospels present him, "Joseph said nothing by his words, but everything by his example." Looking at it from the other direction, I sometimes reflect on how Joseph would have used and not abused the gift of speech.

Which qualities and virtues do I find in Scripture's portrayal of Joseph? If I were to choose just one to imitate, which would it be? How might I apply it?

Novena Prayer to St. Joseph

O St. Joseph, whose protection is so great, so strong,
so prompt before the throne of God,
I place in you all my interests and desires.

O St. Joseph, do assist me by your powerful intercession
and obtain for me from your divine Son all spiritual blessings,
through Jesus Christ, our Lord.
So that, having engaged here below your heavenly power,
I may offer my thanksgiving and homage to the most loving of Fathers.

O St. Joseph, I never weary of contemplating you
and Jesus asleep in your arms.
I dare not approach while he reposes near your heart.
Press him close in my name and kiss his fine head for me,
and ask him to return the kiss when I draw my dying breath.
St. Joseph, patron of departing souls, pray for me.
Amen.

CHAPTER 8

A Father for the Church

"He took care of the Child; he takes care of the Church."
KARL BARTH

The aroma of hot wax from ten thousand candles hits me with a rush as I tug open the heavy doors and step into the stillness. I'm inside the votive chapel at the Oratory of St. Joseph. It adjoins the crypt church beneath the Oratory's massive basilica, which is built on the towering hill that gave Montreal its name. Two million people visit the Oratory every year. For those who come as pilgrims, the votive chapel is a special draw.

Its design—a broad hallway with four large alcoves on each side—invites you to pray and stroll in the company of St. Joseph. Each alcove features a carved wall panel depicting a scene that evokes one of his titles, or patronages. "Model of Workers" catches my eye, and I pause there to light a candle for a relative in an impossible job situation. Moving along, I remember a friend who is discerning between marriage and religious life; she gets prayers and a candle at both "Guardian of Virgins" and "Help of Families." Many people come to mind at "Consolation of the Afflicted" and "Patron of the Dying," and I kneel to pray at both stops.

All around me, other pilgrims are following their own itineraries around the chapel. It's a devout but informal atmosphere—a bit like table-hopping from one group to another at some intimate gathering of family and friends.

At the head table, so to speak, is a large white marble statue of St. Joseph. Centered at the end of the hallway, it sits high on a pedestal-fountain overlooking a ramp of votive lamps. Hands outstretched, palms down as in a blessing—here is St. Joseph, "Patron of the Universal Church." Visually, the ensemble makes a point: this title outranks all the others.

With a Father's Heart

Fr. Roland Gauthier, the St. Joseph scholar who founded the Oratory's research center, confirmed this impression when I met with him later. He explained that St. Joseph's many other titles highlight particular areas where something about his life and person connects with a special need or group of people. Patron of the Universal Church is in a whole different category because it arises from Joseph's unique, God-given mission to be the husband of Mary and the earthly father of Jesus. It's who Joseph *is*.

From Joseph Husband and Father to Joseph Patron of the Universal Church may seem like a mysterious leap of faith, but in reality this aspect of his role was there from the beginning.

Pope Leo XIII gave the classic statement on the subject in his 1889 encyclical on devotion to St. Joseph:

> The divine household, which Joseph governed with a father's authority, contained the beginnings of the new Church. . . . The most holy Virgin is the mother of Jesus Christ; she is also the mother of all Christians. . . . And Jesus is, as it were, the first born of all Christians who have become his brothers by adoption and redemption. . . .
>
> [It follows that Joseph] regards the multitude of Christians who form the Church, the immense family spread over all the earth, as being particularly entrusted to him. Over this family, because he is the husband of Mary and the father of Jesus Christ, he holds a paternal authority. . . . As once he supplied all the needs of the family at Nazareth and watched over it faithfully, so now by his heavenly patronage he protects and defends the Church of Jesus Christ.

Pope St. John Paul II made the point more informally in a homily during a pastoral visit to an Italian diocese in 1993: "The Church is in fact the Body of Christ. Wasn't it therefore logical and necessary that the one to whom the eternal Father confided his Son would also extend his protection over the Body of Christ, . . . the Church?" Four years earlier, he echoed the call of Pope Paul VI to look to St. Joseph not only for our own personal needs but, "in the first place," for the needs of the Church as a whole.

I've felt somewhat convicted as I've examined my conscience about this. In my personal prayer, I do intercede for the Church—for our leaders, for unity, for renewal in the Holy Spirit. But how regular is that prayer? How heartfelt? How informed and guided by the Church? It's so easy to live in a bubble—perceiving the world in a distorted way, preoccupied with my own concerns and those of my little tribe.

Do I pray regularly for the needs of the Church?

Turning to St. Joseph in his role as Patron of the Universal Church is helpful and corrective. It helps to broaden my outlook and turn me outward. Not that I've stopped bringing him my personal needs. But now, St. Joseph's primary title reminds me that my relationship with him is incomplete if it doesn't take account of his concern for the needs of the Church as a whole.

And what might those needs be? There are many to choose from, and probably every Catholic could come up with their own top ten! To whittle it down a bit, let's consider how Joseph protected and nurtured Jesus in his role as his earthly father and how he continues that mission as a spiritual father for the Church.

Joseph, Protector

Joseph kept Jesus alive when Herod was searching "for the child, to destroy him" (Matthew 2:13). The cruel king was a creature of flesh and blood, but behind his scheming lay the diabolical designs of the one who was "a murderer from the beginning" (John 8:44). (This is probably why St. Joseph is invoked as Terror of Demons.)

Diabolical attacks were probably not far from the mind of Pope Pius IX when he declared Joseph Patron of the Universal Church in 1870. Both in the Church and on the political scene, it was a time of tremendous upheaval. Many such times have followed, and later popes have also invoked St. Joseph's help against enemies seen and unseen. Specific challenges change from one papacy to the next, but not the basic need for protection. The Church will always turn to Joseph, said Pope Paul VI, because it is "ever weak, always threatened, and always dramatically in danger." Among those threats, persecution stands out.

As Pope Francis has often stated, more Christians are being martyred for their faith today than during the early centuries of the Church. They are "the bleeding limbs of the body of Christ." One report put their number at four thousand in 2018. Another report for that year estimated that some three hundred million Christians live in a country where they also face other types of persecution: arbitrary arrest, violence, hate crimes, surveillance, and other human rights violations. Hot spots now are South and East Asia, in countries like Myanmar, India, Pakistan, China, and North Korea.

How do I react when I hear that so many Christians are in distress? Pope Francis asked the question at one of his general audiences.

> Am I indifferent, or is it as if one of my family were suffering? . . . Does this touch my heart or not? Am I open to a brother or sister of the family who is giving his or her life for Jesus Christ? . . . Do I pray for my brother, for my sister who is in difficulty because they confess and defend their faith? It is important to look beyond our own boundaries, to feel that we are Church, one family in God!

Here indeed is material for my examination of conscience. And as I reflect on these suffering sisters and brothers in Christ, may their witness encourage me in my own struggles against the world, the flesh, and the devil.

The Needy Human Family

"To look beyond our own boundaries" also means widening our hearts to include anyone in need. This calls for what Pope John Paul II described as a duty and a virtue in his 1987 encyclical on Catholic social teaching: "Solidarity is . . . . a firm and persevering determination to commit oneself to the common good . . . to the good of all and of each individual, because we are all really responsible for all." And so, as he wrote two years later, "those dangers which threaten the human family" are also among the cares that the Church, in a spirit of solidarity, commends to St. Joseph.

Like the dangers facing the Church, the threats to the human family are many. Religious persecution affects not only Christians, but also Muslims, Jews, Hindus, Buddhists, and other members of minority populations around the world. Poverty, war, racism, famine, drought, unemployment, exploitation—the list goes on and on. And, of course, there is abortion, which snuffs out a sacred human life at its very earliest stage.

Considering Joseph's rescue of Mary and the unborn Jesus from Herod's murderous troops, it seems especially fitting to call on him as patron of the unborn. An outdoor shrine by that name—an outreach of the Oblates of St. Joseph in California—features a large statue that invites prayer and evokes this role in a striking way. On a bench sits Joseph, tenderly cradling a six-month-old fetus; opposite him is another bench for quiet meditation. Here, anyone who has lost an unborn child can seek St. Joseph's help for personal healing and, in the case of abortion, God's forgiveness.

One last thought about the flight to Egypt: Joseph's protective mission didn't end once the family had arrived. The Gospels don't say anything about the length of their exile or the dangers they faced, but we can imagine that Joseph had to exercise some courageous creativity to keep his loved ones fed, sheltered, and safe—"like so many of our migrant brothers and sisters who, today too, risk their lives to escape misfortune and hunger," Pope Francis observed. "I consider Saint Joseph the special patron of all those forced to leave their native lands because of war, hatred, persecution and poverty."

Do I share in the Church's concern for all those who are powerless, voiceless, vulnerable? Do I stand up for them by praying and taking action to alleviate their suffering?

Building Up the Body of Christ

Together with Mary, Joseph gave Jesus the best of starts in his life on earth. With great love, he trained his son and passed his knowledge along. He taught Jesus how to handle a hammer, plaster walls, sow seeds, and keep the Sabbath. As Pope Benedict XVI remarked, he exemplifies the core meaning of fatherhood: "to be at the service of life and growth." This mission continues on in the body of Christ, especially in two key areas confided to St. Joseph: evangelization and renewal.

"St. Joseph's patronage must be invoked as *ever necessary* . . . and indeed *primarily*" for the work of proclaiming Christ—both to those who have never heard of him and to those who have neglected or forgotten him. Pope John Paul II could hardly have put it more strongly. Apparently, he saw nothing strange in asking a saint who was a homebody for 99 percent of his life to be the special intercessor for the Church's missionary and apostolic work!

Some Church Fathers also associated Joseph as a missionary as they reflected on how he carried the child Jesus into Egypt. They saw the incident as pointing ahead to the spread of the gospel to the whole world. "Joseph represents the apostles to whom the protection and promotion of Christ is entrusted," St. Hilary wrote in the fourth century.

At least one missionary-minded founder drew inspiration from the thought. Fr. Herbert Vaughan, who began St. Joseph's Missionary Society (also known as Mill Hill Missionaries) in 1866, called Joseph the first missionary to foreign lands. Still today, the Society's primary mission is the pioneering work of bringing Jesus to places where the gospel is unknown.

Joseph's many rooted years of tending the Word in Nazareth also make him a special patron for stay-at-home evangelizers. This includes all of us who aim to make Jesus known and loved through our everyday witness, prayers, and financial assistance. All around us, even in once-Christian settings, there are people who need our witness. Therefore, as Pope John Paul II emphasized, "no believer in Christ can avoid this supreme duty: to proclaim Christ to all peoples." Joseph, who always listened to God's voice and responded courageously to his call, can help us to discover our part in God's redemptive plan.

Am I proclaiming Christ through my example and my words? How can I tell?

Renewing the Church

Just as Joseph nurtured and guided Jesus through his growing-up years, he guides and watches over the Church today. One example is Vatican II, with which St. Joseph has a special connection.

The Second Vatican Council came about through Pope John XXIII's deep devotion to the patron of the Church. "I love him very much," he used to say, and liked to add that his baptismal name was Angelo Giuseppe ("Angel Joseph" in Italian). He would have chosen to go down in history as Pope Joseph

I, he confided, but was concerned that the name might seem too great a break with tradition.

Pope John XXIII's devotion found magnificent public outlet on March 19, 1961, when he issued an apostolic letter proclaiming St. Joseph Patron of the Council, which was to open in October 1962. In view of the need "to obtain from heaven that divine power by which it seems destined to mark an epoch in the history of the Church," wrote the pope, the event "could not be entrusted to a better heavenly protector than St. Joseph, the venerable head of the family of Nazareth and protector of Holy Church."

Pope John could hardly contain his enthusiasm at the thought: "Oh! prayer to St. Joseph! Oh! devotion to St. Joseph for the protection of the Second Ecumenical Council of the Vatican!" It was the first of many urgent requests that every member of the Church bombard St. Joseph with prayer for the council's success.

The Council was indeed a milestone in the history of the Church. It turned to the sources of the Church's life in order to refresh and renew the Church for its mission in the world. The bishops opened the way for greater reading and reflection on Scripture. They enriched the liturgy with forms of the Eucharistic Prayer that echoed the prayers of the ancient church—and made adjustments to encourage a more active participation by laypeople. They repeatedly emphasized the New Testament teaching that all members of the Church are called to follow Jesus as his disciples in their whole lives—and examined what this call means for Christians in the modern world.

In addition, the bishops set the Church on the road toward greater unity with other Christians—and reached out to Jews and adherents of other religions, seeking to overcome hurtful behavior on both sides and to enter into dialogue in a spirit of respect.

Come, Holy Spirit, fill the hearts of your faithful. Inspire in them—in me—the fire of your love.

One of the highest honors that the Catholic Church accords its saints is to mention them during the Mass. Before Vatican II, only Mary, the apostles, and a dozen early martyrs were so honored in the Roman rite. But on November 13, 1962, at one of the Council's general meetings, it was announced that St. Joseph's name would be included in what we know as Eucharistic Prayer I. It reads: "In union with the whole Church we honor Mary, the ever-virgin Mother of Jesus Christ our Lord and God. We honor Joseph, her husband . . ."

This decision, made by Pope John XXIII on his own initiative, was greeted with joy by St. Joseph's many fans around the world. For the Council fathers, though, it came as "a bombshell," says one history of Vatican II. Some objected, because up until then, the Canon was seen as too ancient and holy to tamper with. There were solid theological and pastoral reasons behind Pope John XXIII's action, but he acted when he did because of something he had seen three days earlier, as he followed the Council's debates on closed circuit television.

An elderly bishop from Yugoslavia, Petar Cule, was making a long plea for including St. Joseph's name in the Mass. The audience began to murmur as he nervously rambled on, until finally, the cardinal who was moderating the discussion interrupted with a belittling request to "complete your holy and eloquent speech." It was this treatment of Bishop Cule that prompted Pope John to take action, explained one eyewitness at the Council:

> This caused great astonishment, but few were aware that the pope . . . knew Bishop Cule personally and also knew that his nervous manner of speaking had a tragic source: he had suffered through one of those long trials made famous by the Communists and was sentenced to four years in a concentration camp in Yugoslavia. He and other prisoners were then put on a train which was deliberately wrecked in an attempt to kill all aboard. The bishop survived, but both his hips were broken. In poor health, he had nonetheless made great effort to attend the Council and speak up for St. Joseph. Thus his wish was fulfilled.

The Ready Response of Faith

It's not enough to pray to St. Joseph, said Pope St. Paul VI. "We must also imitate him." There's much to imitate, but one virtue in particular makes Joseph an especially good model for the Church as a whole: his faith.

Quoting one of the Vatican II documents, Pope John Paul II emphasized that "the basic attitude of the entire Church must be 'hearing the word of God with reverence,' an absolute readiness to serve faithfully God's salvific will revealed in Jesus." Joseph, who believed and promptly obeyed God's word received in a dream, shows us what this ready obedience of faith looks like (see Matthew 1:24; 2:14, 21). In Matthew's Gospel, especially, we see what it means for the Church.

Guided by the Spirit, Matthew wrote his Gospel in a way that highlights themes related to the Church and discipleship. You might call it the Church-building Gospel. Jesus as founder of a new community, Peter as its base, expectations for leadership and church life in general—Matthew, more than any other evangelist, put these issues front and center.

We might ask whether his Gospel also puts forward someone who embodies the life of the Church that he shows Jesus founding. Who exemplifies the response to his call to discipleship?

It's not Peter: Matthew recounts Peter's denial of Jesus but doesn't include the later lakeside scene where Peter indicates his repentance (see John 21:15-19). It's not the other apostles: three verses from the end of Matthew, some are still doubting (28:17). And in Matthew, there is no beloved disciple standing faithfully at the foot of the cross. Nor does Matthew replicate Luke's portrayal of Mary as the model follower of Jesus: where Luke focuses on her pondering God's word and persisting in faith, Matthew mentions Mary hardly at all.

Instead, Matthew gives us an opening series of stories whose hero hears and obeys, like the wise man who builds his house on rock (see 7:24). Who more than Joseph exemplifies the response of faith that builds the Church? By placing his example at the very beginning of his Gospel, Matthew offers Joseph as the person to learn from on our own journey of faith.

Prayer for the Church

To you, O blessed Joseph, do we come in our tribulation,
and having implored the help of your most holy spouse,
we confidently invoke your patronage also.

Through that charity which bound you to the Immaculate Virgin Mother of God
and through the paternal love with which you embraced the child Jesus,
we humbly beg you graciously to regard the inheritance
which Jesus Christ has purchased by his blood,
and with your power and strength to aid us in our necessities.

O most watchful guardian of the Holy Family,
defend the chosen children of Jesus Christ.
O most loving father, ward off from us every contagion of error and corrupting influence.
O our most mighty protector, be kind to us
and from heaven assist us
in our struggle with the power of darkness.

As once you rescued the child Jesus from deadly peril,
so now protect God's holy Church
from the snares of the enemy and from all adversity.
Shield, too, each one of us by your constant protection,
so that, supported by your example and your aid,
we may be able to live piously, to die in holiness,
and to obtain eternal happiness in heaven.
Amen.

—Pope Leo XIII

CHAPTER 9

A Family Man

"St. Joseph helped God be a man."
ERNIE (L'ARCHE, CLINTON, IOWA)

No man or woman standing at the altar knows what lies ahead as they pledge fidelity "for better or for worse." They have no way to predict and certainly no way to control future events—no guarantee that the easy will outweigh the difficult. They simply love and rejoice that God has called them to become one.

Like any happy bridegroom, Joseph loved and rejoiced as he welcomed Mary into his home. He couldn't foresee what the future would hold either. By that time, though, he knew that he and Mary would not have the same kind of marriage as the other devout and respectable couples in Nazareth. What would look like an ordinary family would be anything but. His role in it, normal as it might appear from the outside, had no precedent. Father to God's child, husband to a woman consecrated to God in a unique way—in a sense, Joseph would be living as a man with nothing to call his own.

For love of God and love of Mary, he said yes to the whole ensemble. He "took Mary into his home, while respecting the fact that she belonged exclusively to God," Pope John Paul II observed.

He Did It for Love

"Oh, that must have been so hard," we often think as we reflect on what Joseph's "gift of self" entailed—sacrifice, suffering, setting even legitimate desires aside. "Embracing the cross," as I've often heard at wedding homilies (including one where the spouses were told that they would likely *be* each other's crosses).

A total gift of self doesn't come without a struggle, it's true—especially if you haven't been immaculately conceived and aren't free from the effects of original sin. But nothing indicates that Joseph entered into this unusual marriage grimly resigned to a life of daily martyrdoms. He did it for love.

Joseph loved the Lord who had spoken to him through an angel in the night. He loved Mary and wanted her happiness. He had shown that already by searching for a way to separate from her as gently as possible. How relieved he must have been to learn that there was no need to leave her. How his love must have grown as he welcomed her child, conceived by the Holy Spirit—the same Spirit through whom God's love is poured into our hearts (see Romans 5:5).

And how much Mary must have loved Joseph! He believed the incomprehensible reason for her pregnancy, and he showed it by following through with the wedding and acknowledging her child as his own. His yes meant that Mary would be spared the humiliation of an out-of-wedlock pregnancy. Her son would be raised by a man he could call father. She wouldn't have to make her journey of faith alone. Joseph, the strong and tender man she loved, would be her closest friend and partner in mystery and mission.

Perhaps the joy of it moved Mary to break into another *Magnificat*. And perhaps Joseph joined in.

When was the last time I thanked God for the vocation and work he has called me to in this season of life?

Let It Be Done to Us

Pretty much every week, my husband and I have a date night. It's a time for fun and for discussion about our family, but also for doing a reality check on how we're living out our call to become one in the Lord. Over nachos and beer or coffee and dessert, we ask questions like: *So what happened this week? Did we go through things together? Did we draw closer to the Lord? To one another? Where did we fall short? How can we do better?* Usually, after blank looks and a halting start and by the grace of God, we manage to come to something helpful.

I can't imagine that Joseph and Mary had the leisure or the need for a date night. Their relationship went on deepening and deepening, but they were united from the first in the profound intimacy described by spiritual writer Fr. Jacques Leclercq:

> [Marriage is] a complete union, as radical as it can be between human beings, a union which must go down as deep as the human person possesses depth, as far as sharing the same sacrament, as far as being one before God, as far as having the most intimate, the most delicate elements of the interior life and of the supernatural life in common. There is no limit to married intimacy as Christians understand it, and everything in Christian marriage . . . only finds its meaning in a married intimacy which truly brings about the most harmonious and the most complete unity in the partners, the image of the union of Christ and his Church.

We can't know how Mary and Joseph experienced this complete union. Its depths can't be plumbed. From what the Gospels indicate about some events, though, we catch surface glimmers of an intimate collaboration that centered on their unfolding understanding of Jesus' identity. Theirs was a unique child-rearing situation that sometimes called for departing from the usual customs and traditions.

The most obvious and important example is their decision never to have marital relations. How and when they took this approach, no one knows, though it had to have been before they began living together. Neither can anyone know how and when Mary revealed her call to perpetual virginity to Joseph.

For Mary, a life of virginity expressed her wholehearted response of love to the joyful, incomprehensible invitation God had given her. Simply fulfilling the biological and social role of mother wouldn't have fulfilled her desire for total consecration. Mary felt called to another way. "She responds to the proposal of divine love with her own spousal love," John Paul II observed during a general audience in 1996. "Becoming a mother by the power of the Holy Spirit was the form taken by her gift of self."

And out of genuine love for Mary and reverence for the mysterious new thing that God was doing through her, Joseph respected and supported her call. "Through his complete self-sacrifice, Joseph expressed his generous love for the mother of God and gave her a husband's 'gift of self.'"

"Often in life, things happen whose meaning we do not understand," Pope Francis observes. "Our first reaction is frequently one of disappointment and rebellion." Joseph shows another way. "He set aside his own ideas in order to accept the course of events and, mysterious as they seemed, to embrace them, take responsibility for them and make them part of his own history." The spiritual path that Joseph shows us "is not one that explains, but accepts"—with courage and the Holy Spirit's gift of fortitude.

> Just as God told Joseph: "Son of David, do not be afraid!" (Matthew 1: 20), so he seems to tell us: "Do not be afraid!" . . . God always finds a way to carry out his saving plan. . . . God always finds a way to save us, provided we show the same creative

courage as the carpenter of Nazareth, who was able to turn a problem into a possibility by trusting always in divine providence.

By standing with Mary and embracing God's unexpected plan for his life, Joseph advanced God's plan of salvation. In union with Mary's *fiat*, Joseph's "yes" changed the world. How can any of us know what God might do with our own "yes" to his invitations?

How am I giving myself to God?

Unconditional Acceptance

Once Joseph was let in on the secret of Mary's pregnancy, he moved forward with the wedding. This too was a departure from the usual approach. Any other devout Jewish man who discovered that his betrothed was pregnant would have ended the relationship. When Joseph didn't, people in the village would naturally assume that Jesus was his son and that Mary had conceived a little too early. Since betrothed couples were considered legally married, this wouldn't have been wrong, strictly speaking. But it might have been embarrassing.

By accepting Mary unconditionally anyway, Joseph offered Jesus a legitimate place in society and took responsibility for his welfare. This was no small thing in a culture that prized a woman's chastity and legitimate offspring. Before becoming invested in a child, a man wanted assurance that he was really the father. Joseph, knowing without a doubt that he was not, said yes to paternity anyway.

In our world too, we need fathers like Joseph who step up to the plate and take responsibility for children—their own, first and foremost. But perhaps also others whose fathers are deceased, absent, or inattentive. As Pope Francis notes, "Whenever a man accepts responsibility for the life of another, in some way he becomes a father to that person."

Marianist priest Fr. George Montague is one of many who can vouch to that. "You have been a real father to me," he was told by a member-in-training of his religious order, whose father had recently died. Fr. Montague knew what the young man meant. "I could say the same about many others who have fathered me into life as Joseph did for Jesus," he says.

For all men called to paternity—fathers, stepfathers, uncles, adoptive fathers, priests, bishops, and every other kind of spiritual father—Joseph models generous, accepting love. And of course, his example of open-hearted parenting speaks to women as well.

Have I ever experienced embarrassment or humiliation because I did what God called me to do?

He Belongs to You

Jesus brought great joy into Joseph's life. How could it be otherwise? "Already with Mary, and later, especially with Jesus, he began a new way of relating to God, accepting him in his life, entering his project of salvation and doing his will," Pope Benedict XVI said at a 2011 general audience. Assuming his role, Joseph was filled with fatherly delight. St. Bernard imagined it this way:

> He held the Christ Child in his arms and carried him singing lullabies, calmed him if he cried, rocked him in his cradle so that he would fall asleep, spoke baby talk to him, entertained and gave him baby toys, and never returned home without bringing to his little boy Jesus the small birds or little apples or similar things he would find.

A baby's first word, first step, or first tooth—each milestone is joyously noted. As Jesus grew and passed one milestone after another, Joseph and Mary had to put their heads together to discern what to do when traditions or the going wisdom didn't seem to fit what they knew and were learning about their son.

Take that scene in the temple, for example, where Joseph and Mary offer two birds for her ritual purification (see Luke 2:21-24). Certainly, they know what the law of Moses requires. Because every firstborn son is seen as specially set apart for God, he is to be "redeemed"—in a sense, bought back from God, to whom he belonged. It wasn't a complicated procedure, just a monetary payment to a priest. But Luke says nothing about any shekels changing hands at the temple. Despite their strict adherence to the law, however, Mary and Joseph don't redeem Jesus. Instead, they "present him to the Lord." What are they thinking?

Mary and Joseph have concluded that the law calls for something special in the case of this "firstborn male," one commentator suggests. They realize that Jesus is holy in a unique way and that he belongs to God absolutely. Offering the usual redemption payment to "ransom" him from the status of total dedication would make no sense. And so, "they bring Jesus to the temple and present him to God, in effect saying, 'Dear God, here is your Son. He does indeed belong entirely to you.'"

Isn't this an intriguing picture of Joseph and Mary? Without having a full understanding about Jesus, they demonstrate an ability to interpret God's word about him. And together, as it seems, they come to an enlightened approach about how to apply the Mosaic law in a unique situation.

How often, during Jesus' hidden years of growth, they must have had to confer and pray for wisdom about how to raise him. The one episode we have from that period—his finding in the temple—offers a little window into their experience. Most likely, it wasn't the only time that Jesus did something puzzling. On the one hand, they knew Jesus intimately, as you do when you live with someone day-in and day-out. On the other hand, Jesus' full identity and mission were shrouded in deep mystery. There was something about their son that neither parent could quite get.

Joseph and Mary didn't cling possessively to their beloved son. What does this tell me about my own relationships?

Ask for the Grace!

"Who is sufficient for raising children?" every parent wonders. "Not me. I don't have the gifts—not the patience, not the love, not the wisdom . . ."

That's how I felt when I married Kevin. He was a widower with six children; I had been happily single for a long time and was hardly a natural for the role of stepmother. Eager as I was to play my part in this new family configuration, I was often overwhelmed and inclined to thoughts like, "Maybe so-and-so would have been a better choice for Kevin. She's wonderful with kids."

It was a special grace when it dawned on me that Joseph of Nazareth could understand how I felt. He had to exercise authority over two people whose holiness far surpassed his own. Just maybe he hadn't felt up to his role either.

In the Nativity icon known to Eastern Catholics and other Christians of the Eastern churches, Joseph is pictured hunched over in a posture that suggests inner turmoil over Mary's mysterious pregnancy. Sometimes an old man—the devil in disguise—is shown speaking to him, trying to fill him with doubts about Jesus' divine origin.

That icon spoke to me. Although I wasn't fending off the same temptations as Joseph, I was listening to the same voice—to lies that kept me focused on my weakness instead of God's faithfulness and power. I needed to stop fixating on my inadequacies and move forward with trust, as Joseph did.

Joseph accepted the daunting challenge of raising God's only Son—and he met it so well that he's been called the "mirror" or "shadow" of the Father. He trusted that God, who had called him to a unique fatherhood, would give him the gifts to carry it out. He acted on the basis of a principle that St. Thomas Aquinas articulated in reference to Mary: "Those whom God chooses for an office, he prepares and disposes in such a way that they become suited to it."

To everyone who feels cowed and powerless before the challenges they face in their calling, Pope Benedict XVI says:

> God alone could grant Joseph the strength to trust the angel. God alone will give you, dear married couples, the strength to raise your family as he wants. Ask it of him! God loves to be asked for what he wishes to give. Ask him for the grace of a true and ever more faithful love patterned after his own. . . .
>
> Each and every one of us has a role to play in the plan of God. . . . If discouragement overwhelms you, think of the faith of Joseph; if anxiety has its grip on you, think of the hope of Joseph, that descendant of Abraham who hoped against hope; if exasperation or hatred seizes you, think of the love of Joseph, who was the first man to set eyes on the human face of God in the person of the infant conceived by the Holy Spirit in the

womb of the Virgin Mary. Let us praise and thank Christ for having drawn so close to us, and for giving us Joseph as an example and model of love for him.

When has God given me the faith and courage to overcome my fears?

Prayer to Joseph, Husband and Father

Hail, Guardian of the Redeemer,
Spouse of the Blessed Virgin Mary.
To you God entrusted his only Son;
in you Mary placed her trust;
with you Christ became man.

Blessed Joseph, to us too,
show yourself a father
and guide us in the path of life.
Obtain for us grace, mercy and courage,
and defend us from every evil.
Amen.

—Pope Francis

CHAPTER 10

A Working Man

"What's cool about St. Joseph is he didn't perform any miracles. He just stayed home and worked."
JACK BOYLE, AGE 10

One morning, just before diving into the day's work—which was to revise this chapter—I checked to see what the next day's Mass readings would be. I had to laugh when I saw the first verses of the first reading:

> Then Job answered:
>
> "Do not human beings have a hard service on earth,
> And are not their days like the days of a laborer?
> Like a slave who longs for the shadow,
> and like laborers who look for their wages." (Job 6:1; 7:1-2)

Escape from drudgery, from routine—whatever daily work we do, even if we enjoy it—isn't this what most of us long for much of the time? "One minute to five is the moment of triumph," says a receptionist in *Working*, reporter Studs Terkel's classic collection of interviews about jobs and job attitudes. "TGIF," we hear at the end of each work week. "Vacation getaway" ads lure us with promises of adventure and relaxation. So does the dream of early retirement followed by happy golden years of travel, golf, fine dining, and other carefree pursuits.

In our spiritual lives too, we favor the exciting, the routine-breaking. We tend to view Ordinary Time as a filler in the liturgical year. Our taste runs to miracles and drama—to saints like Joan of Arc and Francis of Assisi. Some of their biographies give the impression that they lived on spiritual mountaintops of intense communion with God. Who chooses Br. Benildus as their Confirmation saint? He's the nineteenth-century French schoolteacher whom Pope Pius XI dubbed "the saint of the daily grind."

Put all this together with the fact that what we do most days—that tiring, often monotonous activity we call work—can feel so disconnected from what we do on Sundays, when we go to church and give some attention to our relationship with God. "I often feel overwhelmed and empty on Mondays," says a financial consultant in Arizona. "There are emails and voicemails to follow up on. God takes a back seat because I focus on trying to get through it all." He's gotten intentional about living a more integrated life, though, because "the last thing I want is to start every week with a 'Monday moan' and end it with 'thank God it's Friday' for the next thirty years."

Two Different Worlds

The world that Joseph lived in was less susceptible to this kind of compartmentalization. Especially in the countryside, in villages like Nazareth, piety ran deep. Everyone accepted the basics of Judaism: belief in one God, his covenant with the Jewish people, and the Scriptures; prayer, fasting, and tithing. They gathered for prayer and teaching in the village synagogue (assuming there was one), made pilgrimages to Jerusalem, and observed the Sabbath. They circumcised sons and followed the dietary laws and other rules of purity and impurity. Daily life and religious life were intertwined.

This doesn't mean that every Nazorean lived for God or even had God in mind as they went through the day. As Joseph's son would point out, it's possible to observe the outward forms of religion for the wrong reasons, to honor God with your lips but not your heart (see Matthew 15:18).

Joseph, however, honored God in everything he did. He knew the challenges of the daily grind, but because he was totally surrendered to God, he was schooled in holiness as he exercised his trade. Joseph at the workbench is a picture of "the sanctification of daily life," wrote John Paul II. It's "crucially important" to understand this, he emphasized.

In Joseph, we see that the ordinary activities of work and everyday living can be a high road to holiness. In the ensemble of his life, as in the hidden years of Jesus, seeming opposites are reconciled: prayer and work come together, contemplation and action, the sacred and the secular. It's an aspect of the Incarnation—God affirming and sanctifying the ordinary,

Emmanuel learning and working alongside a simple carpenter. And so, said Pius XII in announcing the feast of St. Joseph the Worker in 1955, "If you wish to be close to Christ, we again today repeat, '*Ite ad Joseph*—Go to Joseph.'"

Do I ever feel close to God as I go about my work and everyday activities? What could I do to become more aware that he is always with me?

Money Matters

Joseph worked hard to meet the physical needs of his family. "I can see him planing, then drying his forehead from time to time," Thérèse of Lisieux imagined in a moment of realism. "How many troubles, disappointments! How many times did others make complaints to good St. Joseph? How many times did they refuse to pay him for his work!"

How much did Joseph earn by the sweat of his brow? The vineyard workers in Jesus' parable received a laborer's daily pay of one denarius. What this is worth in American currency is hard to say, but you might think of it as minimum wage or less. The holy family was poor, though not on the rock-bottom poverty level, scholars say. "Somewhere at the lower end of the vague middle" of the socioeconomic ladder is where a Nazareth woodworker would rank, says John Meier.

Did Joseph have to fight anxiety as he sought to provide for his family? Lacking safety nets like Medicare, Social Security, and pensions, ordinary workers like him lived a more precarious existence than most of us. But Joseph must have faced these worries with trust in God, the great provider. Perhaps Jesus was thinking of his earthly *abba* when he told his disciples: “Do not worry about your life, what you will eat, or about your body, what you will wear” (Luke 12:22).

Joseph’s Job Description

Larry Briskey was just a boy when he started reflecting on how to “go to Joseph.” His friendship with the saint brought great peace to his sixty-eight years of marriage and to his family, he said some years before his death. It began when his attention was caught by a statue of St. Joseph holding Jesus that his mother kept on a pedestal in the hallway. Without quite knowing how to address Joseph, Larry started thinking and reading about him and developed “a great love and respect for his holiness and dedication.” And when Larry did begin to pray to St. Joseph, it felt most natural to begin with work-related issues:

> In my everyday maintenance or building projects, I learned to always pray to St. Joseph for help, especially when I had difficult or even impossible problems in my mechanical tasks. He was always there for me, assisting me. Then, as a retiree, I worked with wood as a hobby, building furniture, mostly. Not having any formal training in cabinetmaking, I depended entirely on St. Joseph for guidance and assistance. Thanks to him, my work began to be in demand. I am very grateful to St. Joseph.

It's understandable that woodworkers like Larry would feel an affinity with the carpenter from Nazareth. So can other people who work with some hard and lasting material. As we saw in chapter 6, *tekton*, the Greek word for Joseph's trade (used in Matthew 13:55 and Mark 6:3) could refer to bricklayers, stonemasons, or even sculptors of marble.

For the woodworking part of his job, Joseph had to be prepared to meet a wide range of needs: simple furniture and storage containers (chests, cabinets, and boxes); agricultural implements (plows, yokes, winnowing fans, and threshing sledges); doors and doorframes, windows and window fittings. He must have done "at least some very skillful and fairly elaborate work," concluded Paul Hanly Furfey in his review of first-century woodworking tools and techniques. Interestingly, most of those tools are similar to those used in colonial America. The hammer, mallet, chisel, saw, drill, plane, lathe, square, and straightedge—all are familiar to us as well.

For the stonework part of the job, "Joseph and Son, Inc." needed muscle as well as technical skill. These projects included terraces, watchtowers, and wine presses. There was house construction and repair, which involved making and positioning heavy roof beams and wrestling foundation stones into place.

"I think Jesus was a rather rugged man, with heavily calloused hands and well-developed muscles," said Scripture commentator George Martin, after visiting an archaeological dig in Israel. Watching a group of muscular young workmen moving a stone from the wall of a first-century house in Bethsaida, he reflected that Jesus might have strained with similar stones. "I don't know whether he was stocky or lanky, but he was strong. He could put in a full day of hard manual work, day after day."

Just like his dad, probably.

Joseph had to work hard for a living. Does the fact that his job included heavy labor adjust my image of him? Of so-called menial laborers?

Calling All Workers

"I figured out what to do," my husband announced triumphantly one busy workday. I was surprised to see his grin and the glint in his eye. Things hadn't been so cheery earlier, when he was struggling with a software issue.

"So how did you figure it out?" I dutifully inquired.

"I prayed to St. Joseph," Kevin answered in dramatic tones. "Remember when I was having that terrible time with the printer yesterday? Well, once I thought of asking St. Joseph to help, I saw what to do. Same thing happened today."

St. Joseph, office technician? It feels like a stretch to connect his overall patronage of work with the kinds of work that so many of us do—jobs that first-century Nazoreans couldn't have begun to imagine. Joseph is a good fit for my cousin Bob, the stonemason. As he was for my uncle Donat, who had bean fields and a dairy farm. Joseph too lived in a rural setting. He probably farmed, certainly had a vegetable garden and kept a few chickens, goats, and maybe a donkey. But what about my friend Jenny, a lawyer? And my son-in-law Freddy, a nurse? What about computer programmers, bus drivers, social workers, journalists, nannies, fast food employees, rocket scientists, and electricians?

All are invited! Everyone who works can look to St. Joseph because of what we have in common with him—not similar job descriptions, perhaps, but the general experience of work. Joseph knew the challenges of working to support his family. He experienced the tiring monotony of the workweek. He faced on-the-job pressures—difficult projects, fussy customers, and late payments. He shared in the universal experience of toil, said Pope St. John Paul II:

> [Toil] is familiar to those doing physical work under sometimes exceptionally laborious conditions. It is familiar not only to agricultural workers, but also to those who work in mines and quarries, to steelworkers at their blast-furnaces, to those who work in builders' yards and in construction work, often in danger of injury or death. It is likewise familiar to those at an intellectual workbench; to scientists; to those who bear the burden of grave responsibility for decisions that will have a vast impact on society. It is familiar to doctors and nurses, who spend days and nights at their patients' bedsides. It is familiar to women, who, sometimes without proper recognition on the part of society and even of their own families, bear the daily burden and responsibility for their homes and the upbringing of their children. It is familiar to all workers, and, since work is a universal calling, it is familiar to everyone.

Fundamentally, then, St. Joseph is the model and intercessor *par excellence* for anyone who works. What can we learn from him?

We Participate in God's Work

From Joseph, we can learn that work is holy. By choosing a carpenter as his earthly father and taking up his trade, Christ enriched human work with an incomparable dignity, John Paul II told a group of factory workers and managers in 1980: "From now on, the one who works knows that he is accomplishing something of the divine, something that can be linked to the initial work of the Creator."

It doesn't always feel that way. Many days, sitting dully at my intellectual workbench, I can't easily connect with this high view of work—*my* work—as a continuation of what began when "God created the heavens and the earth" (Genesis 1:1). But that's the mind-boggling reality.

At the workbench and out on the construction site where Joseph and Jesus labored side by side, "human work was taken up in the mystery of the Incarnation and redeemed in a special way," wrote John Paul II. Pope Francis took up that theme in his 2020 apostolic letter on St. Joseph. Whatever it is that we toil at all day, he said (and I'm broadening this to include unpaid activities like studying, childcare, and watching over elderly relatives), we are "cooperating with God himself and, in some way, become creators of the world around us." Our work becomes "a means of participating in the work of salvation, an opportunity to hasten the coming of the Kingdom, to develop our talents and abilities, and to put them at the service of society and fraternal communion."

For Christians, then, a self-deprecating "I'm just a housewife" or "I'm just a cashier" is hardly an appropriate response to "What do you do?"

Would I approach my work differently if I thought of it as cooperating with God in the ongoing work of creation? What difference might that make to me?

Decent Work for All

This is not to say that every *job* is a good thing. Some exploit. Some lower a worker's dignity by exalting the bottom line and the finished product. Some are hazardous—stressful and carried out in dangerous working conditions. What about people trapped in unpleasant, low-paying jobs—like the chicken eviscerators I worked the night shift with at a processing plant one summer? What about the many who can't find full-time employment and work two part-time jobs but still can't make ends meet?

Unemployment, with all its destructive effects on individuals and families, is hitting record levels in many parts of the world, Pope Francis points out. "How can we speak of human dignity without working to ensure that everyone is able to earn a decent living?"

Dorothy Day, whom the pope held up as a model of good citizenship during his 2015 visit to the US, was asking the same thing decades ago: "What about wages and housing" and the general conditions of poor workers and their families? "Work should be part of heaven, not part of hell," she said after a visit to striking coal miners in western Pennsylvania.

It was to work for social change and to offer help and hospitality to people on the margins that she cofounded the Catholic Worker Movement in 1933. She put all of it under the patronage of St. Joseph, in whom she had the greatest trust. "St. Joseph never fails. He always answers petitions," she wrote supporters after receiving material help for her house of hospitality. "We can go to him now today in thanksgiving and joy and ask him for the same abundance of spiritual favors."

Pope Francis recommends the same as we consider our own response to these great needs. "Let us implore St. Joseph the Worker to help us find ways to express our firm conviction that no young person, no person at all, no family should be without work!"

How do I pray for my work-related needs? How do I express concern for the work-related needs of others?

The Ones Who Go Unnoticed

Writing about St. Joseph during the season of Covid-19 gives a special emphasis to Francis' insistence on the importance of people whose contributions we take for granted in more normal times. There is much to reflect on in his words about these workers whose commitment and essential services came into view during the pandemic:

> We experienced, amid the crisis, how our lives are woven together and sustained by ordinary people, people often overlooked. People who do not appear in newspaper and magazine headlines or on the latest television show, yet in these very days are surely shaping the decisive events of our history.
>
> Doctors, nurses, storekeepers and supermarket workers, cleaning personnel, caregivers, transport workers, men and women working to provide essential services and public safety, volunteers, priests, men and women religious, and so very many others. They understood that no one is saved alone. . . .
>
> How many people daily exercise patience and offer hope, taking care to spread not panic, but shared responsibility. How many fathers, mothers, grandparents, and teachers are showing our children, in small everyday ways, how to accept and deal with a crisis by adjusting their routines, looking ahead and encouraging the practice of prayer. How many are praying, making sacrifices and interceding for the good of all.

Notice that Pope Francis expands the category of "essential workers" to include people we might not have seen in that light: retired persons, parents and grandparents, priests and pastors, teachers, and men and women in consecrated religious life, as well as people who are bedridden, handicapped, or elderly—all who are not physically able to "do" much, but who contribute with their prayers and example.

If, like Joseph, we do it for and with the Lord, all our work is "essential."

Prayer for Everyone Who Works

O St. Joseph, guardian of Jesus, chaste spouse of Mary,
you who spent your life in the perfect fulfillment of duty,
sustaining the holy family of Nazareth with the work of your hands,
kindly protect those who now come to you with trust.
You know their aspirations, their worries, their hopes.
They come to you because they know that you understand and protect them.

You too experienced trials, toil, and weariness.
But even in the midst of concerns about the material needs of this life,
your soul was filled with profound peace and exulted in unfailing joy
through your intimacy with the Son of God, who was entrusted to you,
and with Mary, his most sweet mother.

May those you protect understand that they are not alone
in their work.
May they know how to discover Jesus at their side,
to receive him with grace and to watch over him faithfully,
as you did.

Grant that in every family, in every office, in every laboratory,
and wherever a Christian works, all may be sanctified
in charity, patience, and justice, seeking to do things well
so that abundant gifts may rain down on them from heaven.

Amen.

—Pope St. John XXIII

CHAPTER 11

A Man Who Died Well

"I asked St. Joseph for the grace of a good death for everyone."

St. Bernadette

How and where do you want to die? A friend of mine always said she wanted to die with her boots on. And she did—quite literally—at age seventy-seven, after bundling up to step out into a chill winter evening. In her coat pocket was a prayer card identifying her as a member of the Pious Union of St. Joseph, an association whose members intercede daily for those who are dying.

Cicely Saunders, the British doctor whose strong Christian faith informed her efforts to relieve the pain of people who were terminally ill, hoped to go more slowly: "I'd like to die of cancer because it gives me time to say I'm sorry, and thank you, and goodbye." She died of breast cancer in 2005, working from her sickbed in the hospice she founded, until almost the very end.

We disagree over the manner but not about the goal itself: everyone wants the happy death, the good death, the peaceful death, and death with dignity—the kind of death that Joseph must have had.

The Best of Deaths

We have no particulars about how or when Joseph died. As we saw in the Gospel of Luke, he fades from view after the finding of Jesus in the temple. Luke does seem to imply, however, that when twelve-year-old Jesus returned obediently to Nazareth, he was settling in for the long haul—for "years" of growing in wisdom and grace under both Joseph's and Mary's supervision.

Did Joseph die before Jesus' public ministry? It seems so. Why else would Mary alone be mentioned among the relatives who came looking for Jesus (see Matthew 12:46-50; Mark 3:31-35; Luke 8:19-21; John 2:12)? And if Joseph had been alive when a Cana couple's family gave a wedding feast, he would surely have attended. He would have been with Mary at the cross; there would have been no need for Jesus to entrust her to the beloved disciple's care.

What was the cause of Joseph's death? Was it old age? Did he fall sick? Was he mortally injured on the job? How satisfying it would be if we could read an obituary notice! St. Francis de Sales wouldn't have read one. To him, the cause of Joseph's death was eminently obvious:

> A saint who had loved so much in this life could not die except from love. His soul could not sufficiently love his own dear Jesus amid all the distractions of this life, and he had already performed the services required of him during the childhood of Jesus.
>
> What remained, then, but for him to say to the eternal Father, "O Father, I have accomplished the work which you have given me to do," and then to the Son, "O my Child, as your heavenly Father placed your tender body in my hands on the day you came into the world, so do I now place my spirit in your hands on this day of my departure from this world."

Paintings and statues of the scene depict Joseph expiring peacefully, with Mary at his feet and Jesus at his head, praying for the protection of his soul. It is the best, most consoling of good deaths. For Jesus and Mary, though, the deathbed farewell must have been wrenching. Surrendered though they were to the Father's will, losing Joseph had to be a blow. Besides being their guardian and protector, Joseph was the only person in the whole world who had shared in all the stupendous events of the Annunciation, the Incarnation, and the Nativity. How challenging for Mary especially! Now a widow, she would soon see Jesus leave home.

How does the picture of Mary as a widow and Jesus as a bereaved son speak to me?

A Simple Burial

When someone passes away today, the immediate family is caught up in a whirlwind of activity and decision-making. Contacting funeral home and cemetery, arranging wake and funeral, choosing among a myriad of options: burial or cremation? Top-of-the-line or economy coffin? Open or closed casket? Fancy monument or simple marker? Funeral flowers or "donations preferred"?

The first-century Palestinian approach was simple and quick. We don't know every detail, but at the very least, Joseph's body was washed, anointed with ointments and perfumes, and wrapped in cloth (see Acts 9:37; Matthew 26:12; John 19:40).

If burial followed the usual pattern, it took place on the day Joseph died. Relatives and friends gathered at his home, placed his body on a wooden stretcher (he and Jesus had probably filled orders for many of these in their workshop), and carried it to a gravesite outside the village. The procession was just the kind that Jesus would come across some time later in the town of Nain (see Luke 7:11-14). It wouldn't have been quiet. Funeral etiquette involved wailing, weeping, and singing dirges (see Acts 8:2; Matthew 9:23).

Were any priests present? What official prayers, eulogies, and blessings were said along the way and at the burial place? All we can reasonably assume is that prayers were said and that Jesus played the key part in this and other aspects of Joseph's burial. In this culture, ensuring a proper burial for his parents was a son's special responsibility (see Tobit 6:15). We may not know exactly what services this entailed, but we can be sure that Jesus performed them for Joseph with the greatest love.

Joseph's body was laid to rest—probably in the earth, possibly in a natural cave or tomb hewn out of rock. No one knows where. (A cave discovered in 1889 is sometimes proposed as the site, but there's no evidence that it's authentic.) Burial in the ground was a simple matter of digging a grave. Burial in a family cave or tomb was a two-step process: the body was placed on a ledge in the tomb chamber; after it had decomposed, the bones were gathered up and moved to a pit or an ossuary, a lidded box made of limestone.

Compassion Doesn't Kill

Consoled at death, tenderly cared for after it, and welcomed into heaven with a "well done, my good and faithful servant" (Matthew 25:21, NABRE)—it's no wonder that St. Joseph is known as "patron of a happy death." By extension, he is the "solace of the afflicted" and "hope of the sick," as the litany in his honor calls him. Members of religious orders dedicated to nursing and other types of health care have long considered him their special patron (witness the numerous Catholic hospitals that bear his name). Any caregiver might do the same.

St. Joseph is a special protector for both the unborn, who are at the beginning of life, and for those who are nearing its end. His help is greatly needed. As euthanasia and physician-assisted suicide become more accepted, the risks to life in its final season are increasing.

"I wouldn't ever do it, but seeing my mother and then my father die in so much pain makes you think about calling Dr. Death," our car mechanic told me one day. (He was referring to Dr. Jack Kevorkian, who helped more than a hundred people to end their lives.) "It makes you think . . ."

Human beings have always feared suffering and death. But until the twentieth century, no society tried to address that fear through engineered dying. It's a prideful approach, Orthodox theologian Vigen Guroian observes:

> We have managed to overcome our fear of death enough to seek to manipulate it for our own purposes, to summon it to provide a solution for our personal and social problems. We have overcome our aversion to death enough to get comfortable with using it to get rid of criminals, to end unwanted pregnancies, and, increasingly, to relieve the misery of illness and injury.

"But is there no sanctity in relieving the suffering of others?" asks one euthanasia advocate. Yes, when that "relief" means providing various forms of palliative care; no, when it means disregarding God's sovereignty over life and death and deliberately eliminating the sufferer. As John Paul II explained, "true compassion leads to sharing another's pain; it does not kill the person whose suffering we cannot bear."

In any event, we can't really "get comfortable" with death. Human effort and ingenuity are powerless before this last and greatest enemy. Jesus alone was capable of winning that victory—and he did it for us, through his death and resurrection. "Christ is risen from the dead!" goes the Paschal hymn of Eastern Christians. "By death he trampled death, and to those in the tombs he granted life!"

Doesn't it make sense to turn to Jesus' earthly father as a privileged end-of-life guide and intercessor? He can help us to face death with faith and hope in a way that gives glory to God. Here are a few graces to ask for.

What is the significance for me that Christ is risen from the dead?

The Gift of Peace

There's a healthy and an unhealthy fear of death, spiritual writers tell us. The unhealthy kind is what most of us would most likely develop if we followed techniques like the following, which is taken from a manual of piety for schoolchildren in eighteenth-century France: "As you climb between the sheets, reflect: this linen may one day form my shroud." Also not usually helpful are certain types of moral tales. One classic story, which I heard more than once in my catechism classes, tells of a young person who, on the one day he forgets to wear his scapular, commits a mortal sin and is killed in a car crash.

"There is a kind of good fear which, if handled properly, leads to confidence in God and not to panic," says Benedictine monk Hubert van Zeller. With grace, our "cowardly fear of death" can be changed into a higher "humble fear of punishment for sin," and then into a "fear of offending God" by not offering him our total trust. At that point, says Dom van Zeller, "we find we are not really afraid of death at all. Why not? Simply because we are now leaving the question of our death to him. That is trust. And trust, like love (of which it is an absolutely essential part), casts out fear."

Peace can also come through the intercession of the saints—Mary, of course, whom we invoke in every Hail Mary we pray, and Joseph along with her. In fact, St. Catherine Labouré, the French nun to whom Mary appeared and entrusted the mission of promoting the Miraculous Medal devotion, is said to have requested Joseph's end-of-life intercession for herself.

"Auntie, who should we pray to at the moment of your death?" Catherine's nieces and nephews reportedly asked her one day. "To the 'terror of demons'!" the nun answered. And whenever they faced some temptation, she added, they should pray, "St. Joseph, terror of demons, protect me! And say it on each of your fingers and thumbs!"—ten times, if necessary.

When I think about my own death, what does my reaction reveal about how I relate to God?

The Gift of Meaning and Purpose

There's a mystery about suffering—innocent suffering especially. What purpose does it serve?

While we don't have the full picture, our Christian faith tells us that suffering doesn't diminish the value and dignity of human life. Every life matters to God. "You matter because you are you, and you matter to the last moment of your life," Cicely Saunders would tell her patients as she worked to make their last days comfortable.

And because Jesus won our salvation through an agonizing death on the cross, suffering and death itself have been redeemed. Futile and senseless apart from God, they become meaningful and beneficial—for the sufferer and even for others—when united with the Passion of Christ. While choosing to suffer with Jesus under the sign of the cross doesn't eliminate the pain or the mystery, it is the path to peace and to the hope that does not disappoint. "We suffer *in communion with the Lord*," Cardinal Joseph Bernardin affirmed during his fight with the pancreatic cancer that finally claimed his life in 1996. "And that makes all the difference in the world!"

Indeed it does, says Fr. Guido Gockel, who has administered the Anointing of the Sick at many a bedside in his fifty years as a Mill Hill missionary. As he has often seen, sickness can be an invitation to draw closer to Jesus by sharing in his redemptive suffering: "Through it, we can come to love him more and more"—so much so, "that we may even be able to say, 'O happy sickness, which makes me a partaker in the work of redemption.' This is a grace given to us in the sacrament of Anointing." Like all the sacraments, says Fr. Guido, "it is an encounter with the Lord, who is compassionate and merciful."

Although there's mystery here, you don't have to be advanced in years to grasp and live in this reality of our suffering as redeemed. I think of Carlo Acutis, a cheerful, tech-loving Italian teen who had a deep devotion to the Eucharist. On learning that he had leukemia, Carlo said, "I offer all the suffering I will have to undergo to the Lord, for the pope and the Church." He lived and died at age fifteen (in 2006) with heroic virtue and was beatified in 2020.

Closer to home, I've seen family members and friends who have found meaning in their suffering by accepting it in a context of sacrifice and offering to God. You probably have too. As one of them told me, "It's hard. But in the end, you have to trust that God loves you and knows what he's doing with you."

To Live and Die by Faith

"You will not die," the serpent assured Eve. Eat this forbidden fruit and "you will be like God" (Genesis 3:4, 5). The sin of our first parents—the desire to usurp authority over our own lives that belongs to God, afflicts us still. A "certain Promethean attitude," John Paul II called it—a mindset that "leads people to think that they can control life and death by taking the decisions about them into their own hands."

It takes humility to see ourselves as creatures—to surrender our illusion of control and live and die by faith, as Joseph did. This is no easy sacrifice.

I saw something of the struggle and the victory in the life of a friend who was diagnosed with early-onset Alzheimer's disease when she was in her mid-fifties. Myriam really wrestled with God over this, but eventually she accepted—and even embraced—this cross, for love of him.

I'll never forget the last time we talked. Her speech and memory were going, and she was just barely coherent, but she wanted to share what had become her favorite prayer. I could hardly hold back the tears as I saw what it was: St. Ignatius of Loyola's *Suscipe*, which begins: "Take, O Lord, and receive all my liberty, my memory, my understanding." Now *that's* humility.

Do I think of myself as belonging to God, who created me? Does the way I live reflect how I see myself in relation to God?

Memento Mori

"The thought of death, perhaps very near, certainly not far away, brings me back to my beloved St. Joseph." Pope St. John XXIII was eighty when he made this entry in his spiritual journal in 1961. It wasn't the first time he had thought about death, nor the first time he had considered it in the company of St. Joseph, his "first and beloved protector."

Reflecting on our own death from time to time, as he did, can be a valuable spiritual practice. It can motivate us to seek first the kingdom of God, to pursue the treasures that really matter in life. And if we do this in a spirit of faith and trust in our Father, who sent his only Son to save us and fill us with his own Holy Spirit, it doesn't have to be grim. John XXIII, who especially recommended this practice in the company of St. Joseph, was the jolliest pope ever.

From St. Joseph, patron of a good death, we can learn to live well so as to die well. With his gentle direction, we can approach death in the spirit that writer Henri Nouwen recommended to his friend Cardinal Bernardin: "People of faith, who believe that death is the transition from this life to eternal life, should see it as a friend."

Prayer for Those Who Are Close to Death

O St. Joseph, foster father of Jesus Christ and true spouse of the Virgin Mary,
pray for us and for those who will die this day (or night).

—Prayer of the Pious Union of St. Joseph

Prayer for a Happy Death

O blessed Saint Joseph,
you gave forth your last breath
in the loving embrace of Jesus and Mary.
When the seal of death closes my life,
come with Jesus and Mary to aid me.

Obtain for me this solace for that hour:
to die with their holy arms around me.

Jesus, Mary, and Joseph,
I commend my soul living and dying,
into your sacred arms.
Amen.

—The Oblates of St. Joseph

CHAPTER 12

Portrait of a Family

"I don't know how one can think about the Queen of Angels and about when she went through so much with the Infant Jesus without giving thanks to St. Joseph."

ST. TERESA OF AVILA

Every now and then, our friend Jim would show up alone for the Sunday liturgy. Usually he attended with an entourage—his wife, Linda, and their four children. "It feels strange to be here alone," he'd say whenever he came solo. It seemed strange to us too—not that we failed to appreciate Jim as a person in his own right. It's just that we were used to seeing him in context, with his wife and family.

Although we don't see Jim or his family any more since our move to a different part of the country, his remark is on my mind as I think about St. Joseph. Important as it is to get to know him on an individual basis, we miss something crucial if we don't see him in connection with Jesus and Mary. In fact, our devotion to him will go wrong if examining his close-up doesn't lead us to a deeper appreciation of the family portrait.

Joseph's most devoted and enthusiastic cheerleaders have known this. St. André Bessette, who saw himself as "St. Joseph's little dog," had such confidence in the saint's fatherly intercession that he counseled everyone to turn to him for every kind of healing and help. But Brother André taught too that devotion to St. Joseph should never be separated from devotion to Jesus and Mary.

For St. Francis de Sales, who also had a special love for Joseph, the members of the holy family were inseparable. In a prayerful address to Mary, he said, "It is impossible not to picture beside you, in a place of honor, one whom your Son in his love for you so often graced with the title of father." We find the same insistence in the writings of St. Teresa of Ávila, whose innovative way of relating to St. Joseph as her father marked a milestone in the history of devotion to him.

More recently, Pope St. John Paul II is just one of the many leaders of the Church who have sounded the theme:

> Just as we cannot speak of Jesus without referring to his most holy mother, so we cannot speak of Jesus and Mary without recalling him who, through an authentic, although very particular, form of paternity, had the task of serving as "father" to the Son of God.

Joseph Emerges

Imagine paging through a photo album and finding a family picture in which one member is blurry, faded, or just barely in view. Imagine too that the blurriness is symbolic—that it represents your lack of knowledge about the person in question.

How much easier it would be to appreciate the group as a whole if you knew the identity and character of the mysterious personage. The interplay of individual personalities is such an important factor in determining the unique quality and flavor of a family's life. How much more you appreciate that flavor if you're acquainted with each member of the family and know something of how they all relate to one another.

For a long time in the history of the Church, the picture of the holy family was like that incomplete photo in the family album. From the first, Jesus stood out in bold relief. Relatively quickly, his light illumined Mary, revealing her singular dignity as mother of God.

But until the late Middle Ages, the earthly head of this unique family was just a dim, peripheral figure. And because Joseph was hidden in the shadows, devotion to the family as a whole was also slow to develop. "The image of St. Joseph as an active, full-fledged participant in the holy family had to be established before it was possible to consider Jesus, Mary, and Joseph as forming an integral and credible family unit," explains Fr. Joseph Chorpenning, whose research on the subject is illuminating.

Credit for this restoration goes first to Jean Gerson (1363–1429), an energetic and influential chancellor at the University of Paris. Reacting against the apocryphal portrayal of Joseph as a doddering caretaker, Gerson insisted instead on his youth, vigor, and important role as husband and father in the holy family.

Following the trail blazed by Gerson, some of the Italian artists of the Renaissance also challenged the view of "old

Joseph." Artists of the Middle Ages almost always depicted him as elderly, bearded, and bald. Neither did they make him stand out in any way. He was just a sideline character in scenes of Jesus' birth and infancy, his importance downplayed. "The least saint of our provinces had his statue," observes art historian Émile Mâle. "St. Joseph did not have his."

Renaissance paintings of Joseph showed him in a different light. The Italian artists agreed with Gerson that Joseph must have been younger and more vigorous than his traditional portrayals. How else could he have withstood the rigors of a trek to Egypt and years of heavy labor as a carpenter? they reasoned. An early example of how they saw him is Raphael's 1504 "Marriage of the Virgin," which features a thirtyish Joseph.

St. Joseph's new look took root a bit later in Spain, once St. Teresa of Ávila's writings had begun circulating. They made the country into "the chosen land of St. Joseph," notes Émile Mâle. El Greco, Zurbarán, and especially Murillo, "the painter of St. Joseph," picture the saint as a strong man in the prime of life. Handsome too! In paintings by the "new style" artists, Joseph's face resembles the face of the adult Christ.

"Why must we think that Joseph was ugly?" St. Teresa's coworker, Fr. Jerónimo Gracián, asked in an influential work about the saint. Written in 1597 at the request of a group of Roman carpenters, his *Summary of the Excellencies of St. Joseph* was a thoughtful, creative culling from earlier writers that quickly became the most widely circulated book on St. Joseph in Europe. As a result, devotion to him surged in Italy and Spain.

What's my picture of St. Joseph? How does it affect the way I relate to him?

Trials and Tribulations

As various writers have noted, this recapturing of St. Joseph's true significance—along with the unfolding development of devotion to the holy family—took place during a historical period when the ordinary family was especially at risk. Plague, war, famine, economic distress—in the face of such dangers, it made sense to turn to the holy family and to its protector and provider, St. Joseph.

It was in the nineteenth century, another period of crisis for families, that devotion to the holy family really burst into bloom. The industrial revolution was shifting economic activity away from the home and into the factory, which raised huge issues about work time, fair wages, and child labor, to name only a few. New laws and a new spirit of selfish individualism threatened the family as an institution.

Pope Leo XIII, who had encouraged devotion to St. Joseph in 1889, was deeply concerned about these developments. He responded to them in his best-known encyclical, *Rerum Novarum* (1891), which set the course for Catholic social teaching. And as an "on the ground" way to strengthen families, he did all he could to encourage devotion to Jesus, Mary, and Joseph. An apostolic letter he wrote in 1892 has been called "the *magna carta* of the Holy Family devotion in modern times." We also have Pope Leo to thank for the Feast of the Holy Family, which we now celebrate on the Sunday after Christmas (or on December 30).

Today's challenges to the family are no less daunting than they were in earlier times. Some are familiar; some are new. Pope John Paul II noted some of the newer varieties in his 1994 "Letter to Families":

> Various programs backed by very powerful resources nowadays seem to aim at the breakdown of the family. At times it appears that concerted efforts are being made to present as "normal" and attractive, and even to glamorize, situations which are in fact "irregular." Indeed, they contradict "the truth and love" which should inspire and guide relationships between men and women, thus causing tensions and divisions in families, with grave consequences especially for children. The moral conscience becomes darkened; what is true, good, and beautiful is deformed; and freedom is replaced by what is actually enslavement.

More recently, in "The Joy of Love" (2016), Pope Francis opened with a summary of challenges to the family that were discussed at the preceding synod of bishops. It's quite a list. Here's a sampling, in no particular order: pornography, consumerism, abortion, drug use, reproductive technologies, poverty, absentee parents, sexual exploitation, issues of gender identity, immigration, divorce, selfish individualism, domestic abuse, state interventions such as forced sterilizations and abortions, unemployment, challenges to the view of marriage as the exclusive and indissoluble union between a man and a woman, the weakening of faith and religious practice, the lack of affordable housing, the lack of supports for parents, for families caring for the elderly, or for members with special needs. And the list goes on. Each of us could add to it.

But Pope Francis ended the summary with a helpful reminder not to get "trapped into wasting our energy in doleful laments, but rather [to] seek new forms of missionary creativity" that offer truth and hope. Pope John Paul did just that when he repeatedly urged all members of the Church to work towards a "civilization of love"—a culture built on our free and total gift of self to God.

Jesus made that gift in a supreme way by emptying himself and dying on the cross so that the Father's plan of salvation could be fulfilled. Mary made that gift with her *fiat*. Through his connection with her, so did Joseph. The holy family, with the child at the center, is at the heart of the transformation that the world and our own families need today. The way forward? Keep our eyes on Jesus, says Pope Francis:

> The mystery of the Christian family can be fully understood only in the light of the Father's infinite love revealed in Christ, who gave himself up for our sake and who continues to dwell in our midst. I now wish to turn my gaze to the living Christ, who is at the heart of so many love stories, and to invoke the fire of the Spirit upon all the world's families.

What helps me when I'm feeling discouraged about my own family's struggles? Where do I turn? What would it mean for me to turn my gaze on Jesus and invoke the fire of the Holy Spirit?

A Few Family Pictures

Like the Trinity and like the Church, the family is above all a communion of persons. It's meant to be a sign and image of the loving relationship that unites the three Persons of the Trinity.

A "Mystical" Picture

Some spiritual writers expressed this by explicitly presenting Joseph, Jesus, and Mary as a sort of "earthly trinity" representing the mystery of Father, Son, and Holy Spirit. As evidenced by numerous paintings of "the heavenly and earthly trinities" in the religious art of Canada, Latin America, and Europe, artists also found this idea congenial.

In their images, there's a heavenly realm where God the Father, the dove of the Holy Spirit, and angels dwell. Below it, in the earthly realm, stands the Christ Child, flanked by Mary and Joseph. The two trinities—one vertical, one horizontal—intersect in the Jesus, who brings heaven and earth together.

A Real-Life Picture

Perhaps more in the spirit of the Incarnation are those representations of the holy family in which the heavenlies remain veiled. It's an ordinary scene: a husband, a wife, and a child. But for Maria von Trapp and others, this is the picture with power to amaze:

> Men have founded orders, congregations, and organizations; God's own foundation is the Christian family. A real mother, a real father, and a real Child, living, loving, suffering—not symbols, but people like us. . . . That means that instead of having a "devotion to the Holy Family," we must treat the Holy Family in a way as our next-door neighbors, become acquainted with them, go visiting, invite them over, watch them all the while, and ponder about them in our hearts.

A Personal Picture

Whenever St. Teresa of Ávila thought of the holy family, she saw herself as part of it. Her response came naturally. Her mother died when Teresa was eleven, and the girl turned to Mary as her mother. Joseph came into her life in a special way when she was twenty-one and suffering from a mysterious, debilitating illness. She attributed her healing to his intercession: St. Joseph, "being who he is, brought it about that I could rise and walk and not be crippled," she explains in her autobiography.

Teresa rediscovered "the incarnation of the Infant Jesus, of Mary, of Joseph, as living human beings, with whom one could speak on familiar terms, who answered you, who were interested in you," observes one spiritual writer. She wanted everyone to know they could that they could experience that too.

A Wide-Angle Picture

The name "Joseph" means "may God add"—that is, "may God give us more children just like this one." Scripture scholar Joseph Fitzmyer imagines Joseph's father and mother exulting over their newborn son and deciding to name him Joseph as an expression of their delight. It's a happy thought.

Perhaps we can build on it by taking Joseph's name as an encouragement to view ourselves in an even bigger family picture. The spiritual writer and mystic Adrienne von Speyr (1902–1967) points in that direction in this observation about Joseph and his family:

> They do not simply live a life of pleasure and joy in one another. They live there already for the Christians to come, for us. The house at Nazareth is no closed house, nor a closed paradise; it has doors and windows that open out into the Church.

The holy family is hospitable. It's not closed in on itself. It invites the weary traveler in—to learn, to rest, to be fed, and to receive strength and support for the journey.

Perhaps, then, there are *three* pictures to ponder as we reflect on Joseph and his family. There's the close-up of the holy trio, in which St. Joseph is blurry no more. There's the one that shows you with them. And finally, there's the super-wide-angle shot that zooms out to show the multitudes gathered around the little family of Nazareth.

Jesus, Mary, Joseph—and me, and you, and everyone who has been drawn into the communion of life and love in the body of Christ. Look at it closely and the portrait of the holy family isn't an image of only three persons. It's a miniature of the entire Church in mission to the world.

What does it mean for me that I'm invited to enjoy an intimate relationship with Joseph and his family?

Prayer for the Family

Jesus, Mary and Joseph,
in you we contemplate the splendor of true love.
To you we turn with trust.
Holy Family of Nazareth, grant that our families too
may be places of communion and prayer,
authentic schools of the Gospel and small domestic churches.

Holy Family of Nazareth,
may families never again experience violence, rejection and division.
May all who have been hurt or scandalized find ready comfort and healing.
Holy Family of Nazareth, make us once more mindful
of the sacredness and inviolability of the family,
and its beauty in God's plan.
Jesus, Mary, and Joseph,
graciously hear our prayer.
Amen.

—Pope Francis

Sources and Notes

Numbers on the left refer to pages in the text.

Introduction: Joseph the Unnoticed

14 *apostolic letter*: Pope Francis, *Patris Corde* (With a Father's Heart), http://www.vatican.va/content/francesco/en/apost_letters/documents/papa-francesco-lettera-ap_20201208_patris-corde.html

15 *took care of the child*: Francis L. Filas, SJ, "Barth as Seeker of God's Truth," *The Christian Century*, May 30, 1962, 686.

16 *the man who goes unnoticed*: Pope Francis, *With a Father's Heart*, Introduction.

17 *Each of us can discover in Joseph*: Pope Francis, Introduction.

Chapter 1
Joseph the Perplexed

For chapters 1 and 2 on the Gospel of Matthew, in addition to the cited sources, I drew insight and information from:

Raymond E. Brown, SS, *The Birth of the Messiah*, Anchor Bible Reference Library (New York: Doubleday, 1993).

Joseph A Fitzmyer, SJ, *Saint Joseph in Matthew's Gospel: St. Joseph's Day Lecture, March 21, 1997* (Philadelphia, PA: St. Joseph's University Press, 1997).

George Martin, *Bringing the Gospel of Matthew to Life*, Opening the Scriptures Series (Frederick, MD: The Word Among Us Press, 2008).

19 Nat Hentoff, *John Cardinal O'Connor: At the Storm Center of a Changing American Catholic Church* (New York: Charles Scribner's Sons, 1987), 34.

20 *"the essential theology…":* Advent preaching: Raymond E. Brown, SS, *A Coming Christ in Advent*, (Collegeville, Minnesota: Liturgical Press, 1988), 19.

25 *Basil, Jerome, and other Church Fathers:* Francis L. Filas, SJ, *Joseph: The Man Closest to Jesus* (Boston: St. Paul Editions, 1962), 144-25.

29 *"readiness of will":* John Paul II, *Redemptoris Custos* (Guardian of the Redeemer), 4, http://www.vatican.va/content/john-paul-ii/en/apost_exhortations/documents/hf_jp-ii_exh_15081989_redemptoris-custos.html.

30 *wick, reed:* John P. Meier, *A Marginal Jew, vol. 1*, Anchor Bible Reference Library (New York: Doubleday, 1991), 321.

30 *Cistercian prayer*: *Proclaiming All Your Wonders: Prayers for a Pilgrim People* (Collegeville, Minnesota: Liturgical Press), 136–37.

Chapter 2
Joseph the Hero

31 *he conquered himself:* Joseph F. Chorpenning, OSFS, *Just Man, Husband of Mary, Guardian of Christ: An Anthology of Readings from Jerónimo Gracián's "Summary of the Excellencies of St. Joseph (1597)"* (Philadelphia: St. Joseph's University Press, 1993), 173.

35 *John Chrysostom:* Filas, *Joseph: The Man Closest to Jesus,* 385–386.

38 *the Old Testament Joseph:* Kevin and Louise Perrotta, *Genesis 37–50: Joseph the Dreamer*, Six Weeks with the Bible Series (Chicago: Loyola Press, 2004).

40 *Joseph as just:* Brown, *Coming Christ,* 39; Donald Senior, *Matthew*, Abingdon New Testament Commentaries (Nashville: Abingdon Press, 1998), 40.

40 *sleeping Joseph prayer*: Donald H. Calloway, MIC, *Consecration to St. Joseph* (Stockbridge, MA: Marian Press, 2020), 247.

Chapter 3
Joseph the Silent

42 Paul Claudel, *Positions et propositions*, vol. 2 (Paris: Gallimard, 1932), 149, quoted in Roland Gauthier, CSC, "St. Joseph in the History of Salvation," in *St. Joseph and the Third Millennium,* ed. Michael D. Griffin, OCD (Hubertus, WI: Teresian Charism Press, 1999), 271.

42 Romano Guardini, *The Lord,* trans. Elinor Castendyk Briefs (Chicago: Henry Regnery Company, 1954), 13.

43 Georgina Sabat-Rivers, *Sor Juana Inés de la Cruz and Sor Marcela de San Félix: Their Devotion to St. Joseph as the Antithesis of Patriarchal Authoritarianism,* Saint Joseph's Day Lecture, March 21, 1996 (Philadelphia: Saint Joseph's University Press, 1997), 18.

47 *one who has been graced*: John S. Custer, *The Holy Gospel: A Byzantine Perspective* (Pittsburgh: God With Us Publications, 2004), 422.

47 *Mary's social status:* Luke Timothy Johnson, *The Gospel of Luke*, Sacra Pagina Series (Collegeville, MN: Litugical Press, 1991), 39.

47 *she might have to think of herself differently*: George Martin, *Bringing the Gospel of Luke to Life*, Opening the Scriptures Series (Huntington, Indiana, Our Sunday Visitor, 2011), 20-21.

49 *postdated commands*: Kevin Perrotta, *Mary: Jesus' Mother—and Ours*, Six Weeks with the Bible Series (Chicago, Loyola Press, 2011), 17.

49 *interpretations of Mary's question*: Raymond E. Brown, SS, *The Birth of the Messiah*, Anchor Bible Reference Library (New York: Doubleday, 1993), 303–07. Custer, *The Holy Gospel*, 423; Joseph A. Fitzmyer, SJ, *The Gospel according to Luke, I–IX*, 348-50; Martin, *Luke*, 22–24.

50 *Bernard of Clairvaux:* John McHugh, *The Mother of Jesus in the New Testament* (London: Darton, Longman & Todd, 1975), 66.

52 *prayer: St. Joseph, Come to Help Us*, University of Dayton, accessed March 18, 2021, https://udayton.edu/imri/mary/p/prayer-saint-joseph-come-to-help-us.php.

Chapter 4
Joseph the Faithful

54 Alfred Delp, S.J., *Prison Writings*, Modern Spiritual Masters Series, (Maryknoll, NY: Orbis Books, 2004), 63.

56 *firstborn:* Fitzmyer, *Luke,* 407–408.

57 *Justin Martyr, cave*: Fitzmyer, *Luke*, 408.

62 *Jews expected the Messiah to conquer Gentiles:* Martin, *Luke,* 73–74.

63 *Jerusalem population and Passover crowds:* Rami Arav and John J. Rousseau, *Jesus and His World* (Minneapolis: Augsburg Fortress, 1995), 163.

67 *Prayer in honor of Joseph's joys and sorrows:* Filas, *Joseph: The Man Closest to Jesus,* 641–642. [abridged and slightly adapted].

Chapter 5
Joseph, Who Are You?

69 *St. John of the Cross:* André Doze, *Joseph: Shadow of the Father,* trans. Florestine Audett, R.J.M. (New York: Alba House, 1992), 36.

70 *Matthew and Luke on the birth of Jesus:* Joseph A. Fitzmyer, SJ, *Saint Joseph in Matthew's Gospel: St. Joseph's Day Lecture, March 21, 1997* (Philadelphia: St. Joseph's University Press, 1997), 7–10. Larry M. Toschi, OSJ, *Joseph in the New Testament* (Santa Cruz, California: Guardian of the Redeemer Books, 1991), 90–97.

71 *genealogy theories:* Brown, *Messiah,* 504, 588.

72 *God put himself in history:* Pope Francis, homily, December 17, 2013.

73 *on force-fitting Matthew and Luke:* Martin, 40.

74 *the brothers and sisters of Jesus:* Filas, *Joseph: The Man Closest to Jesus*, 77–102; Fitzmyer, *Luke,* 723–724; Joseph T. Lienhard, S.J., *St. Joseph in Early Christianity* (Philadelphia: St. Joseph's University Press, 1999), 16–19; *Mary in the New Testament,* eds. Raymond E. Brown, Karl P. Donfried, et al. (Philadelphia: Fortress Press; New York: Paulist Press, 1988), 65–72; John McHugh, *The Mother of Jesus in the New Testament* (London: Darton, Longman & Todd, 1975), 200–254.

74 *hidden stream of tradition:* Perrotta, *Mary*, 56.

74 *Origen*, Epiphanius, Jerome: Lienhard, *St. Joseph in Early Christianity*, 16–19.

77 All of the apocryphal writings mentioned can be found in *The Apocryphal New Testament,* ed. J.K. Elliott (Oxford, England: Clarendon Press, 1993).

77 Tarcisio Stramare, O.S.J., *Gesù lo chiamò Padre* (Città del Vaticano: Libreria Editrice Vaticana, 1997), 21–26;

77 *Joseph as aged widower:* McHugh, *The Mother of Jesus*, 218.

77 *Protogospel of James: Apocryphal New Testament*, 57–67.

78 *genuine historical details:* Fitzmyer, 110.

79 *Infancy Gospel of Thomas*: *Apocryphal New Testament,* 75–83.

80 *real husband, real father:* Information on these subjects is drawn from Lienhard, *St. Joseph in Early Christianity*, 19–26; Filas, *Joseph: The Man Closest to Jesus*, 103–33, 165–231; Gauthier, "St. Joseph in Early Christianity," in *Third Millenium*, 275–80.

81 *guardian of the divine mystery:* Pope John Paul II, *Guardian of the Redeemer*, 5.

83 *a true fatherhood:* Pope John Paul II, 21.

84 *person and mission of Jesus:* Pope John Paul II, 7, 8.

85 *Byzantine prayers*: Metropolitan Cantor Institute of the Byzantine Catholic Archeparchy of Pittsburgh, accessed March 18, 2021, https://mci.archpitt.org/menaion/12-26-31-Sunday.html.

Chapter 6
An Ordinary Nazorean

In addition to the cited sources, material for this chapter is from:

David Noel Freedman, ed., *The Anchor Bible Dictionary*, vols. 1–6, (New York: Doubleday, 1992).

Seán Freyne, *Galilee: From Alexander the Great to Hadrian* (Wilmington, DE: Bloomsbury T & T Clark , 1998).

Catherine Hezser, ed., *The Oxford Handbook of Jewish Daily Life in Roman Palestine* (New York: Oxford University Press, 2010).

86 *Thérèse of Lisieux: Her Last Conversations,* trans. John Clarke, OCD (Washington, D.C.: ICS Publications, 1977), 159.

91 *the older the individual:* Bruce J. Malina, *Windows on the World of Jesus: Time Travel to Ancient Judea* (Louisville, KY: Westminster John Knox Press, 1993), 35.

93 *occupations:* John Pilch, "Anyone unwilling to work should not eat," *The Bible Today* (January 1994): 38–45; John Riches, *The World of Jesus* (Cambridge: Cambridge University Press, 1990), 25; Meier, *A Marginal Jew,* 280–285; Rami Arav and John J. Rousseau, *Jesus and His World* (Minneapolis: Augsburg Fortress, 1995), 339–341.

95 *scribal literacy:* Meier, *A Marginal Jew*, 278.

95 *steadfast interiority*: Pope Benedict XVI, Angelus, St. Peter's Square, Fourth Sunday of Advent, December 18, 2005, http://www.vatican.va/content/benedict-xvi/en/angelus/2005/documents/hf_ben-xvi_ang_20051218.html.

95 *in the rhythm of the days:* Pope Benedict XVI, General Audience, December 28, 2011, http://www.vatican.va/content/benedict-xvi/en/audiences/2011/documents/hf_ben-xvi_aud_20111228.html.

96 *prayer to St. Joseph, guardian of families:* Fr. Antony Vazhappilly, pastor, St. James the Apostle Catholic Church, Fremont, California, February 25, 2021, https://sjapostle.net/?p=1375.

Chapter 7
A Friend in High Places

98 Karl Rahner: Karl Rahner, S.J., "A Homily for the Feast of St. Joseph," in *Third Millenium*, 338.

98 *Cheryl Scheidel story*: used with permission.

99 *a living Body:* Edward D. O'Connor, CSC, *The Catholic Vision* (Huntington, IN: Our Sunday Visitor, 1992), 436. Also 434–438 on honoring and praying to the saints.

102 *all our needs:* Teresa of Ávila, *The Book of Her Life*, in *The Collected Works of St. Teresa of Ávila 1*, trans. Kieran Kavanaugh, OCD, and Otilio Rodriguez, OCD (Washington, DC: Institute of Carmelite Studies Publications, 1976), 53.

102 *workmen:* Chorpenning, *Just Man*, 243–44.

102 *Brother André:* Bernard La Freniere, CSC, *Brother André According to Witnesses.* (Montreal: Oratory of St. Joseph, 1992), 86–7.

103 *when affluent people:* Benedict J. Groeschel, CFR, *A Still, Small Voice* (San Francisco, CA: Ignatius Press, 1993), 88, 90.

103 *on burying St. Joseph statues:* Stephen J. Binz, *St. Joseph, My Real Estate Agent* (Ann Arbor, Michigan: Servant Publications, 2003).

104 *adorned with every virtue:* Chrysostom, quoted in Filas, *Joseph: The Man Closest to Jesus,* 383–4.

104 *patron of priests:* Edward Jealy Thompson, *The Life and Glories of St. Joseph* (Rockford, IL: Tan Books, 1980), 442.

105 *Fr. Larry Richards*: "St. Joseph, A Man of Our Times," Archdiocese of Detroit virtual men's conference, July 25, 2020, https://detroitcatholic.com/news/daniel-meloy/follow-st-joseph-in-times-of-crisis-fr-larry-richards-tells-local-catholic-men-video.

106 *novena prayer:* If you ignore the "never been known to fail" guarantee that often comes with this prayer, says Joseph scholar Fr. Francis Filas, this is "actually a very reasonable and humble prayer." *St. Joseph after Vatican II* (Youngstown, Arizona: Cogan Productions, 1981), 41.

Chapter 8
A Father for the Church

107 Francis L. Filas, S.J., "Barth as Seeker of God's Truth," 686.

108 *Joseph as Patron of the Universal Church:* Gauthier, "St. Joseph in the History of Salvation," in *Third Millenium,* 281–88.

109 *divine household:* Pope Leo XIII, *Quamquam Pluries*, August 15, 1889.

109 *Pope John Paul II*: March 19, 1993 homily, *L'Osservatore Romano,* English ed. (March 24, 1993), 7.

109 *in the first place:* Pope John Paul II, *Guardian of the Redeemer*, 30.

111 *Pope Paul VI:* March 19, 1969, talk, *L'Osservatore Romano,* English ed. (March 27, 1969), 1.

111 *Pope Francis on today's martyrs*: "Pope Francis Invites Prayers for People Persecuted for Their Religion," Vatican News, compiled by Sr. Bernadette M. Reis, August 22 and 23, 2020.

111 *persecution of Christians:* Statistics from "Christian Persecution," *Aid to the Church in Need*, accessed March 18, 2021, https://www.churchinneed.org/christian-persecution; "Harassment of Religious Groups Continues to Be Reported in More Than 90% of Countries," Pew Research Center, November 10, 2020, https://www.pewforum.org/2020/11/10/harassment-of-religious-groups-continues-to-be-reported-in-more-than-90-of-countries/.

112 *am I indifferent?* Pope Francis, general audience, September 25, 2013, http://www.vatican.va/content/francesco/en/audiences/2013/documents/papa-francesco_20130925_udienza-generale.html.

112 *Solidarity is:* Pope John Paul II, *Sollicitudo Rei Socialis* (The Concern of the Church for the Social Order), 38, http://www.vatican.va/content/john-paul-ii/en/encyclicals/documents/hf_jp-ii_enc_30121987_sollicitudo-rei-socialis.html.

112 *dangers which threaten the human family:* Pope John Paul II, *Guardian of the Redeemer*, 31.

113 *Shrine of St. Joseph:* 544 West Cliff Drive, Santa Cruz, California; shrinestjoseph.com

113 *migrant brothers and sisters:* Pope Francis, *With a Father's Heart*, 5.

114 *to be a father*: Pope Benedict XVI, Vespers address in Cameroon, March 18, 2009, http://www.vatican.va/content/benedict-xvi/en/speeches/2009/march/documents/hf_ben-xvi_spe_20090318_vespri-yaounde.html.

114 *patronage must be invoked:* Pope John Paul II, *Guardian of the Redeemer*, 29, emphasis mine.

114 *St. Hilary: The Fathers of the Church: St. Hilary of Poitiers Commentary on Matthew,* trans. D.H. Williams (Washington, D.C.: Catholic University of America Press, 2012), 48.

114 *Fr. Herbert Vaughan and Mill Hill:* Edward V. Casserly, S.S.J., "Devotion to St. Joseph in the Josephite Society in the United States," *Cahiers de Joséphologie* (1955): 589. Information on the Mill Hill Missionaries: millhillmissionaries.com.

115 *to proclaim Christ to all peoples:* Pope John Paul II, *Redemptoris Missio* (Mission of the Redeemer), 3.4, 30.1, http://www.vatican.va/content/john-paul-ii/en/encyclicals/documents/hf_jp-ii_enc_07121990_redemptoris-missio.html.

115 *Pope John XXIII: Le voci*, March 19, 1961, quoted in *Cahiers de Joséphologie* IX (July-December 1961): 163, 164; Filas, *Joseph: The Man Closest to Jesus,* 627.

118 *Bishop Petar Cule:* Xavier Rynne, *Vatican Council II* (Farrar, Straus, & Giroux, 1968), 75–76.

118 Eucharistic Prayers II, III, and IV: following up on an action approved by Pope Benedict XVI, Pope Francis decreed the insertion of St. Joseph's name into these prayers as well.

118 *Pope Paul VI*: Angelus, March 19, 1970, *L'Osservatore Romano,* English ed. (March 26, 1970), 3.

119 Pope John Paul II, *Guardian of the Redeemer*, 30.

120 *Leo XIII prayer:* at the end of *Quamquam Pluries,* August 15, 1889. As shown on the U.S. Bishops' website: https://www.usccb.org/prayer-and-worship/prayers-and-devotions/prayers/prayer-to-st-joseph-after-rosary.

Chapter 9
A Family Man

Especially helpful sources of ideas and information for this chapter:

George Martin, *Bringing the Gospel of Matthew to Life* (Frederick, MD: The Word Among Us Press, 2008).
George Martin, *Bringing the Gospel of Luke to Life* (Frederick, MD: The Word Among Us Press, 2011).
Kevin Perrotta, *Luke: The Good News of God's Mercy*, Six Weeks with the Bible Series (Chicago, IL: Loyola Press, 2000).
Kevin Perrotta, *Mary: Jesus' Mother—and Ours* (Chicago, IL: Loyola Press, 2011).

122 *Ernie:* Christella Buser, *Flower from the Ark: True Stories from the Homes of L'Arche* (Mahwah, New Jersey: Paulist Press, 1996), 38.
123 *took Mary into his home:* Pope John Paul II, *Guardian of the Redeemer*, 20.
125 *Fr. Jacques Leclercq: Marriage: A Great Sacrament,* trans. the Earl of Wicklow (Dublin: Clonmore and Reynolds, 1951), 53.
126 *Mary responds with spousal love:* Pope John Paul II, May 1, 1996 general audience, *L'Osservatore Romano*, English ed. (May 8, 1996).

126 *his generous love:* Pope John Paul II, *Guardian of the Redeemer*, 20.

126 *our reaction of disappointment and rebellion:* Pope Francis, *With a Father's Heart*, 4.

127 *paternity concerns:* Bronislaw Malinowski, *Sex, Culture, and Myth* (New York: Harcourt, Brace & World, 1962), 63.

128 *responsibility for the life of another:* Pope Francis, *With a Father's Heart*, 7.

128 George T. Montague, SM, *Companion God: A Cross-Cultural Commentary on the Gospel of Matthew* (New York: Paulist Press, 1989), 23.

129 *Pope Benedict XVI:* General Audience, December 28, 2011.

129 *St. Bernard:* as reported by Gracián in Chorpenning, *Just Man*, 132.

129 *redeemed*: Martin, *Luke*, 66–67.

130 *the presentation of Jesus:* Perrotta, *Mary*, 63–4.

132 *shadow, mirror:* Doze, *Shadow of the Father*, 17.

132 *Thomas Aquinas:* Filas, *Joseph: The Man Closest to Jesus*, 386.

132 *Pope Benedict XVI:* Homily in Cameroon, March 19, 2009.

132 *prayer:* Pope Francis, end of *With a Father's Heart*.

Chapter 10
A Working Man

134 *Jack Boyle:* from a private conversation.

134 Studs Terkel, *Working: People Talk About What They Do All Day and How They Feel About What They Do* (New York: Pantheon Books/Random House, 1972), 31.

135 *Benildus:* Ann Ball, *Modern Saints: Their Lives and Faces* (Rockford, Illinois: Tan Books, 1983), 40.

135 *the Monday moan:* Brad Prose, "The Slight Pause," Christians in Commerce, accessed March 21, 2021, https://www.christiansincommerce.org/christ-alive/slight-pause.

136 *Joseph at the workbench:* Pope John Paul II, *Guardian of the Redeemer*, 22, 24.

137 Pius XII, "Feast of St. Joseph the Workman," *The Catholic Mind*, September 1955, 564.

137 *Thérèse of Lisieux: Last Conversations*, 159.

137 *Joseph's earnings*: Paul Hanly Furfey, SJ, "Christ as Tekton," *The Catholic Biblical Quarterly* 17 (1955): 213–214.

138 Meier, *A Marginal Jew,* 282.

138 *Larry Briskey:* story used by permission.

139 Paul Hanly Furfey, SJ, "Christ as *Tekton,*" 204–215.

139 George Martin, *God's Word* (Huntington, IN: Our Sunday Visitor, 1998), 15.

141 *Toil is familiar:* Pope John Paul II, *Laborem Exercens* (On Human Work), 9.2, http://www.vatican.va/content/john-paul-ii/en/encyclicals/documents/hf_jp-ii_enc_14091981_laborem-exercens.html.

142 *to factory workers:* John Paul II, talk to Olivetti workers, March 19, 1980, *L'Osservatore Romano,* English ed. (March 24, 1980), 12.

142 *human work*: Pope John Paul II, *Guardian of the Redeemer*, 22.

143 *our work gives us an opportunity:* Pope Francis, *With a Father's Heart*, 6.

144 *human dignity:* Pope Francis, *With a Father's Heart*, 6.

144 *what about wages?* Dorothy Day, "The Church and Work," *The Catholic Worker*, September 1946, 1, 3, 7, 8, *Catholic Worker* online archives: https://www.catholicworker.org/dorothyday/articles/154.html.

144 *work should be part of heaven:* Dorothy Day, "Reflections on Work," December 1946, 1,4, *Catholic Worker* online archives: https://www.catholicworker.org/dorothyday/articles/229.html.

144 *St. Joseph never fails:* Dorothy Day, "May Day," May 1956, 2, *Catholic Worker* online archives: May 1956, https://www.catholicworker.org/dorothyday/articles/704.html.

144 *implore St. Joseph the Worker:* Pope Francis, *With a Father's Heart*, 6.

145 *our lives are woven together:* Pope Francis, *With a Father's Heart*, Introduction.

146 *prayer:* John XXIII, Radio Message to workers on the Feast of St. Joseph the Worker, May 1, 1960, https://www.vatican.va/content/johnxxiii/it/messages/pont_messages/1960/documents/hf_j-xxiii_mes_19600501_lavoratori.html [my translation].

Chapter 11
A Man Who Died Well

148 *Bernadette:* Doze, *Shadow of the Father,* 66.

148 Sheryl Gay Stolberg, "Dame Cicely Saunders: Reflecting on a Lifetime of Treating the Dying," *The New York Times*, May 11, 1999, F 7.

150 Francis de Sales, *Treatise on the Love of God* 2, trans. John K. Ryan (Rockford, Illinois: Tan Books, 1974), 49.

151 *death and funeral rites:* Raymond E. Brown, *The Death of the Messiah* 2 (New York: Doubleday, 1993), 1243–1265.

152 *tombs:* Jack Finegan, *The Archeology of the New Testament: The Life of Jesus and the Beginning of the Early Church* (Princeton: Princeton University Press, 1992), 292–318.

153 Vigen Guroian, *Life's Living toward Dying* (Grand Rapids, Michigan: William B. Eerdmans Publishing Company, 1996), 16.

153 *true compassion leads to sharing:* Pope John Paul II, *Evangelium Vitae* (The Joy of the Gospel), 66.2, http://www.vatican.va/content/john-paul-ii/en/encyclicals/documents/hf_jp-ii_enc_25031995_evangelium-vitae.html.

154 *manual of piety:* John McManners, *Death and the Enlightenment* (Oxford: Clarendon Press; New York: Oxford University Press, 1981), 199.

154 Dom Hubert van Zeller, *Death in Other Words* (Springfield, Illinois: Templegate, 1963), 13–14.

155 *terror of demons*: Sr. Emmanuel, *The Hidden Child* (Mayfield, Pennsylvania, PA: Hutchinson Co., 2007), 257.

156 *Cicely Saunders*: "Obituary: Dame Cicely Saunders," BBC News, July 14, 2005, http://news.bbc.co.uk/2/hi/uk_news/4254255.stm.

156 *in communion with the Lord:* Joseph Bernardin, *The Gift of Peace* (Chicago: Loyola Press, 1997), 47.

157 *Anointing of the Sick:* Fr. Guido Gockel, MHM, *I'm On My Way* (Kindle edition, March 5, 2020), 46–7.

157 *Carlo Acutis:* Angela Mengis Palleck, "Millenial Generation Has A Blessed," Vatican News, October 10, 2020, https://www.vaticannews.va/en/church/news/2020-10/carlo-acutis-blessed-assisi- eucharist-patron-internet.html.

157 *Promethean attitude:* Pope John Paul II, *Humanae Vitae* (Of Human Life), 15.3, http://www.vatican.va/content/paul-vi/en/encyclicals/documents/hf_p-vi_enc_25071968_humanae-vitae.html.

158 Pope John XXIII, *Journal of a Soul,* trans. Dorothy White (New York: McGraw-Hill Book Company, 1965), 318, 344.

159 *death as a transition:* Bernardin, *The Gift of Peace*, 127–128.

159 *Pious Union prayer*: piousunionofstjoseph.org. "To live well so as to die well" was a favorite saying of St. Louis Guanella (1842–1915). The Pious Union, one among many good works of his, is an international association of people who pray for the suffering and dying. In the US: Pious Union of St. Joseph for the Suffering and Dying, 953 East Michigan Avenue, Grass Lake, Michigan 49240.

159 *Prayer for a happy death:* Filas, *Joseph: The Man Closest to Jesus*, 648.

Chapter 12
Portrait of a Family

Much of this chapter has been inspired by the cited works of Fr. Joseph Chorpenning.

161 *St. Teresa of Ávila:* Joseph F. Chorpenning, OSFS, *The Holy Family in Art and Devotion* (Philadelphia: St. Joseph's University Press, 1998), 28.

162 *St. André Bessette*: Henri-Paul Bergeron, CSC, "La dévotion à saint Joseph chez le frère André," *Cahiers de Joséphologie* (June-July 1975): 54, 47. On Brother André, see also Henri-Paul Bergeron, *Brother André, The Wonder Man of Mount Royal* (Montreal and Paris: Fides, 1958); Bernard LaFreniere, CSC, *Brother André According to Witnesses* (Montreal: St. Joseph's Oratory, 1997).

162 *St. Francis de Sales*, *Treatise on the Love of God,* trans. Vincent Kerns, MSFS (Westminster, MD: Newman Press, 1962), xxv.

162 Pope John Paul II, "The Church Needs Joseph's Bold Faith for New Evangelization," *L'Osservatore Romano* (September 22, 1993), 4.

163 Joseph F. Chorpenning, OSFS, *The Holy Family Devotion* (Montreal: Center for Research and Documentation, Oratory of St. Joseph, 1997) 4.

164 *Emile Mâle:* Robert Boenig, ed., *The Mystical Gesture: Essays on Medieval and Early Modern Spiritual Culture in Honor of Mary E. Giles* (Oxfordshire, UK: Taylor & Francis, 2018).

164 *Gracián on Joseph's looks:* Chorpenning, *Just Man*, 111.

166 *magna carta:* Chorpenning, *Holy Family Devotion, 56.*

166 *Letter to Families:* Pope John Paul II, *Letter to Families, 5*, http://www.vatican.va/content/john-paul-ii/en/letters/1994/documents/hf_jp-ii_let_02021994_families.html.

166 *challenges to the family:* Pope Francis, *Amoris Laetitia* (Joy of Love), 32–57, http://www.vatican.va/content/francesco/en/apost_exhortations/documents/papa-francesco_esortazione-ap_20160319_amoris-laetitia.html.

167 *wasting our energy:* Pope Francis, *Amoris Laetitia*, 57.

167 *civilization of love*: Pope John Paul II, *Letter to Families*, 14.

167 *mystery of the Christian family:* Pope Francis, *Amoris Laetitia*, 57.

168 *earthly trinity in art:* Chorpenning, *Holy Family in Art*, 85.

169 Maria von Trapp, *Yesterday, Today, and Forever* (Philadelphia, PA: Lippincott, 1952), 47.

169 *Joseph, being who he is*: Chorpenning, *Holy Family in Art,* 26.

170 *Teresa of Ávila and the Holy Family:* Doze, *Shadow of the Father,* 36.

170 *on the name Joseph:* Fitzmyer, *Joseph in Matthew's Gospel*, 2.

170 *Adrienne von Speyr:* Chorpenning, *Holy Family Devotion,* 67.

171 *Prayer for the Family*: Pope Francis, Angelus, December 29, 2013, http://www.vatican.va/content/francesco/en/angelus/2013/documents/papa-francesco_angelus_20131229.html.